Jesus Wasn't Killed by the Jews

D1601152

Jesus Wasn't Killed by the Jews

Reflections for Christians in Lent

Edited by
Jon M. Sweeney

Foreword by
Rabbi Abraham Skorka

Afterword by
Amy-Jill Levine

ORBIS BOOKS
Maryknoll, New York

ORBIS BOOKS
Maryknoll, New York 10545

Founded in 1970, Orbis Books endeavors to publish works that enlighten the mind, nourish the spirit, and challenge the conscience. The publishing arm of the Maryknoll Fathers and Brothers, Orbis seeks to explore the global dimensions of the Christian faith and mission, to invite dialogue with diverse cultures and religious traditions, and to serve the cause of reconciliation and peace. The books published reflect the views of their authors and do not represent the official position of the Maryknoll Society. To learn more about Maryknoll and Orbis Books, please visit our website at www.orbisbooks.com.

Names: Sweeney, Jon M., 1967- editor. | Skorka, Abraham, 1950-
    writer of foreword. | Levine, Amy-Jill, 1956- writer of afterword.
Title: Jesus wasn't killed by the Jews : reflections for Christians in Lent
    / edited by Jon M. Sweeney ; foreword by Rabbi Abraham Skorka ;
    afterword by Amy-Jill Levine.
Description: Maryknoll, NY : Orbis Books, [2020] | Includes
    bibliographical references. | Summary: "Christian and Jewish
    scholars respond to the role of Gospel texts (particularly Lenten
    readings) in fostering anti-semitism"-- Provided by publisher.
Identifiers: LCCN 2019035554 (print) | LCCN 2019035555 (ebook) |
    ISBN 9781626983526 (paperback) | ISBN 9781608338177 (ebook)
Subjects: LCSH: Jesus Christ--Passion--Role of Jews. | Christianity
    and antisemitism. | Lent--Meditations.
Classification: LCC BT431.5 .J47 2020 (print) | LCC BT431.5 (ebook)
    | DDC 261.2/6--dc23
LC record available at https://lccn.loc.gov/2019035554
LC ebook record available at https://lccn.loc.gov/2019035555

To Lawrence Kushner,
my first rabbi, friend, and mentor

Contents

Antisemitism Yet Again

Rabbi Abraham Skorka

On May 4, 2019, I received an invitation from Jon M. Sweeney to prepare a foreword for a book entitled *Jesus Wasn't Killed by the Jews*. The immediate catalysts for this book were the attacks on the synagogues in Pittsburgh, Pennsylvania, and Poway, California, in October 2018 and April 2019. The reappearance of blatant antisemitism in American society caused heartache for many, Jews and non-Jews alike. Could the murders of these members of worshiping Jewish congregations herald further perils that Jews could have to face in this country?

Jon, as a Catholic, took the initiative of responding to the root cause of much antisemitism over the centuries: the Christian allegation that Jews collectively were guilty of the crucifixion of Jesus, their own Messiah. The idea of this book, to consider the long-lived image of Jews as deicides, made me recall the complex and ambivalent attitudes that Catholics had toward the Jews during the twentieth century with terrible consequences.

In the last century, when the darkening clouds of racist antisemitism began covering Europe, some members of the Catholic Church (inspired by a converted Jewish woman, Sophie Franziska van Leer) founded the *Opus sacerdotale Amici Israel* (Priestly Association of Friends of Israel). One of the aims of the organization, which included 19 cardinals, 278 bishops and archbishops, and approximately 3,000 priests, was to change Catholic attitudes toward Jews. A primary objective was to introduce changes into the Good Friday liturgy during which the Jews were described as "perfidious." They presented the issue to Pope Pius XI in early 1928, and received the Holy Father's answer through a decree that he approved on March 22, 1928. He rejected any changes to the liturgy, but declared: "Ruled by the same charity, the Apostolic See has protected this people against unjust vexations, and just as it reproves all hatred between peoples, so it condemns hatred against the people formerly chosen by God, the hatred that today customarily goes by the name of antisemitism."[1]

Rebutting Jewish criticism of this Vatican resolution,[2] Enrico Rosa, SJ, the publisher of *La Civiltà Cattolica*, insisted on a difference between racial antisemitism and anti-Judaism. The first is rejected by the church, he argued; the second is accepted. In an article entitled "Anti-Semitismus" for the *Lexikon für Theologie und Kirche*, Gustav Gundlach, SJ, wrote similarly.

Along with Gustave Desbuquois, SJ, and John LaFarge, SJ, Gundlach was one of the drafters of a proposed encyclical that Pope Pius XI intended to issue. Although the pontiff died without responding to the draft, or perhaps even reading it, it propounded the same distinction between racism (which it rejected) and religious anti-Judaism (which it endorsed). One of the purposes of this prospective papal text, to criticize the discrimination, persecutions, and violence suffered by European Jews at the beginning of 1939,[3] was undermined by this religiously based antipathy. The hate against Jesus's supposed killers was thus a barrier that separated Christians from Jews. In the Christian religious consciousness, Jews were allies of the devil.

In summer 1942, when the annihilation of the Polish Jews entered its critical stage, a Polish Catholic writer, Zofia

---

1. The references here presented about the *Amici Israel* and their efforts to change the Good Friday liturgy were taken from the second chapter of Hubert Wolf's book *Pope and Devil: The Vatican's Archives and the Third Reich*, trans. Kenneth Kronenberg (Cambridge, MA: Harvard University Press, 2010).

2. *Jewish World*, April 16, 1928.

3. Frank J. Koppa, "Pope Pius XI's 'Encyclical' *Humani Generis Unitas* Against Racism and Anti-Semitism and the 'Silence' of Pope Pius XII," *Journal of Church and State* 40, no. 4 (1998): 775–95.

Kossak-Szczucka, published a declaration under the title "Protest!" (Remonstrance). She called on her Polish fellows to save their Jewish neighbors from death. In that document, we read the following paragraphs that depicted the contradictory sentiments of a Catholic writer, even though she had a great commitment to displaying Christian virtues toward her Jewish neighbors:[4]

> The world is looking at these atrocities, the most horrible throughout the whole history of mankind, and is silent. The slaughter of the millions of people is happening in ominous silence. The executioners are silent, they do not boast about what they are doing. England is silent, so is America, even international Jewry is silent, before so sensitive to all harm to their people. Silent are Poles. Polish political friends of Jews limit themselves to journalistic notes, Polish opponents of Jews show no interest in a matter that is alien to them. Dying Jews are surrounded only by Pilates washing their hands. Silence shouldn't be tolerated anymore. If for no other reason—it is mean. Those who are silent in the face of murder—become partners of the killer. Those who do not condemn—approve.
>
> . . . Our feelings toward Jews have not changed. We do not stop thinking about them as political, economic and ideological enemies of Poland. Moreover do we realize that they still hate us more than Germans, that they make us co-responsible for their misfortune. Why? On what basis? It remains the secret of the Jewish soul. Nevertheless, it is a fact that is continuously confirmed. Awareness of those feelings doesn't relieve us of the duty to condemn the crime.

She goes on to affirm:

> We also know how poisoned the fruit of the crime is. The role of forced observer of the bloody spectacle taking place

---

4. Extracted from http://marcuse.faculty.history.ucsb.edu/classes/33d/projects/church/ChurchZegotaRachel.htm.

on Polish soil might promote immunity to pain and suffering and, what is the most important, the conviction that to murder your neighbor without any punishment is permissible. Those who do not understand it and want to connect the proud and free future of Poland with contentment in the face of the grief of fellow human beings is neither a Catholic nor a Pole.

Zofia Kossak-Szczucka was cofounder of the Council to Aid Jews (*Rada Pomocy Żydom*), code named Żegota, the underground organization for the rescue of Jews in Poland. In 1985 she was posthumously named "Righteous among the Nations" by Yad Vashem.

Regarding Kossak-Szczucka's "Protest," Robert D. Cherry and Annamaria Orla-Bukowska wrote in the introduction to *Rethinking Poles and Jews*: "Without at all whitewashing her antisemitism in the document, she vehemently called for active intercession on behalf of the Jews—precisely in the name of Polish Roman Catholicism and Polish patriotism."[5]

Her ambivalent attitude is a terrible example of the confusion produced through the transmission of an ambivalent message of love and hate.

The *Shoah* perpetrated against the Jewish people in the midst of Europe raised a painful question for European culture at large and for the Christian churches in particular. What was the contribution of almost twenty centuries of anti-Judaic Christian theology to this horrible crime, unique in human history? The crime had such proportions, the cruelty manifested was so terrible that the foundations of Christianity itself trembled.

It was a Jew who lost his wife and daughter in the *Shoah* who was one of the first to take steps after the war to close the gap between Christians and Jews. He understood that the values Jews and Christians hold in common must be reasserted for the sake of humanity and that Jews and Christians must begin a new and positive stage in the history of their relations. This

---

5. Robert Cherry and Annamaria Orla-Bukowska, *Rethinking Poles and Jews: Troubled Past, Brighter Future* (Lanham, MD: Rowman & Littlefield, 2007), 5.

had to be done to the utmost in order not to let Nazism achieve a posthumous victory by destroying the Judeo-Christian component of European culture. The key to open the new way, he understood, was to disassemble antisemitism by correcting the Christian teaching that had prevailed for so long that "the Jews" had killed Jesus. His name was Jules Isaac.

Isaac was a greatly respected historian and educator who supervised the French educational curricula from which generations of students learned about history. As an assimilated Jew who had been confronted by the darkest manifestations of inhumanity during the *Shoah*, he was spiritually impelled in 1943, after the deportation of his wife and daughter, to research Christian teaching about Jesus in order to combat Christian anti-Judaism, the substratum of Nazi antisemitism. The book, *Jesus and Israel*, is divided into four parts in which he tries to provide, through a rigorous historical method, an accurate image of Jesus and his life.

He dedicated his book with these words: "In MEMORIAM. To my wife and my daughter. Martyrs. Killed by Hitler's Nazis. Killed. Simply because their name was ISAAC."[6]

Part 4 of the book offers several propositions about "The Crime of Deicide." At the beginning of Proposition 16, as an introduction to the theme, he wrote:

> For eighteen hundred years it has been generally taught throughout the Christian world that the Jewish people, in full responsibility for the crucifixion, committed the inexpiable crime of deicide. No accusation could be more pernicious—and in fact none has caused more innocent blood to be shed.[7]

After learning of the deaths of his wife and daughter in Auschwitz, Jules Isaac continued working on his research after the end of the Second World War. He was one of the most impor-

---

6. Jules Isaac, *Jesus and Israel*, trans. Sally Gran (New York: Holt, Rinehart & Winston, 1971).

7. Ibid., 233.

tant thinkers who contributed to the 1947 "Seelisberg Conference," which issued a famous declaration of "Ten Points" for
reforming Christian teaching.[8]

On June 13, 1960, he met with Pope John XXIII, urging him to
include the issue of Jewish–Catholic relations as a topic for the
Second Vatican Council, which he had announced six months
earlier. John XXIII, who during the war had saved thousands
of Jews from the Nazis' murderous hands, was deeply affected
by Isaac's request. He shortly after directed Cardinal Augustin
Bea, SJ, to prepare the draft for a conciliar statement to forge a
new path in Jewish–Catholic relations.[9] This was the beginning
of a long and meandering process that ended with the declaration *Nostra Aetate* being approved by a vote of the assembled
bishops of the council of 2,221 ayes against 88 nays. It was pro-
mulgated by Pope Paul VI on October 28, 1965.

Since then much has been done and important advances
have been made. Popes John Paul II, Benedict XVI, and Francis
have taken large and courageous steps. Nevertheless, the way
ahead for Jews and Christians is still long and filled with challenges to be overcome.

In the conclusion to his book, Isaac wrote:

> Anti-Judaism will retain its virulence as long as the Chris-
> tian Churches and peoples do not recognize their initial
> responsibility, as long as they do not have the heart to
> wipe it out. Latent antisemitism exists everywhere, and
> the contrary would be surprising: for the perennial source
> of this latent antisemitism is no other than Christian reli-
> gious teaching in all its forms, the traditional and tenden-
> tious interpretation of Scripture, the interpretation which
> I am absolutely convinced is contrary to the truth and love
> of him who was the Jew Jesus. The Jewish problem is not

---

8. Christian Rutishauser, "The 1947 Seelisberg Conference: The Foundation
of the Jewish-Christian Dialogue," *Studies in Christian–Jewish Relations* 2, no. 2
(2007): 34–53.

9. John Connelly, *From Enemy to Brother: The Revolution in Catholic Teaching on the Jews, 1933–1965* (Cambridge, MA: Harvard University Press, 2012),
240–41.

only a temporal problem; it is first and fundamentally a spiritual problem, whose resolution can be found only in a profound spiritual and religious renewal.[10]

The renewal to which he refers is the dramatic message that cries out from Auschwitz demanding a commitment to a process of change in which human hate no longer has the power to transform earthy reality into a hell. Isaiah 66:22 says: "For the new heavens and the new earth which I make are standing in front of Me, says the Lord, so shall stand your seed and your name." Rabbi David Kimchi (Narbona, Provence, 1160–1235) explains that the verse is not referring to a re-creation of the cosmos by God, but rather to a new human reality in which the seed of all those who kept the values of dignity in the past will be present. According to the biblical vision, this new reality will be made not only by the Creator, but also by human efforts and contributions.

This book was prepared with this vision in mind. May the Almighty bless the intentions of its authors so that they and their descendants will be present in a better reality, that dreamed of by Jesus and by Jules Isaac.

Saint Joseph´s University,
Philadelphia, July 18, 2019,
the day of the twenty-fifth
anniversary of the bombing
of the building of the Jewish
Community of Buenos Aires
(AMIA). Let this text be a trib-
ute to the memory of all those
who were killed there.

---

10. Isaac, *Jesus and Israel*, 400 n. 6.

INTRODUCTION

We Need This Book

JON M. SWEENEY

As Rabbi Skorka writes in his foreword, this book was conceived in the weeks after the shooting at a synagogue in Poway, California, about twenty miles north of San Diego. That tragedy (April 27, 2019) was the latest in a series of attacks on Jewish people, carried out by people calling themselves Christians, who seem to believe they are acting on behalf of their faith, in support of the cause of Christ.

In Poway, a young man with a semiautomatic rifle entered a Chabad congregation on the last day of Passover, and began firing where approximately one hundred people were attending services. The shooter was only nineteen years old. He knew none of the people he was trying to kill—except that they were likely Jewish. Two people died and several were injured; many more would have died if the teenager's gun hadn't jammed and he hadn't fled the scene. This all took place six months to the day of an even worse synagogue shooting inspired by antisemitism at the Tree of Life synagogue in the Squirrel Hill neighborhood of Pittsburgh, Pennsylvania. You can look these things up, if you don't remember them. There will be others.

It is easy to dismissively say that the perpetrators of such crimes are insane. *They are obviously out of their minds,* we say. If they didn't often defend themselves specifically as Christians, that would be an easy explanation for their behavior. It is becoming clearer, sadly, with each new tragedy, that these madmen have often reasoned their way to their murderous behavior. There is, in fact, a long tradition within Christianity to do so.

As for expressing their Christian faith in the killing of Jews, the perpetrators obviously couldn't be more wrong, when considering the central tenets of our faith. But then this book wouldn't be necessary if the "obviously" in that sentence was accurate. It isn't.

Many Christians have been taught antipathy toward Jewish people as a kind of faithfulness to the Christian gospel. For example, the shooter in Poway was a member of a local Presbyterian church. He'd posted a "manifesto" in explanation of what he was about to do hours before entering the synagogue; it was posted on a social media website, and its language was a blend of Bible quotations and white nationalist rhetoric. In the days following the attack and the suspect's arrest, thousands of Christians were involved in discussions on social media about Christianity's role in these abhorrent views. One prominent pastor in the Presbyterian church remarked that the shooter's writing presented "a frighteningly clear articulation of Christian theology" and warned: "There's a deep and ugly history of anti-Semitism that's crept into the Christian church, that needs to be continuously addressed, condemned and corrected."[1]

There are many, many other historical examples of similar actions and viewpoints. Some of these are offered in the essays to come; so I won't repeat them all here. You will hear of great historical figures, theologians and teachers of the faith, who included in their teaching and preaching the denigration of Jewish people, even characterizations of Jews as evil or less than human, as if Christian tradition rests on such ideas. And then there are passages from our Scriptures that are, at least, troubling, such as John 8:42–44: "Jesus said to them, 'If God were your Father, you would love me, for I came from God and now I am here. I did not come on my own, but he sent me. Why do you

---

1. Reverend Duke Kwon, quoted in Julie Zauzmer, "The alleged synagogue shooter was a churchgoer who talked Christian theology, raising tough questions for evangelical pastors," *Washington Post*, May 1, 2019.

not understand what I say? It is because you cannot accept my word. You are from your father the devil'" (NRSV). So why are we surprised that a young man of college age, who was reared in the church, would shoot at Jews in a synagogue?

* * *

Christians have been taught our faith as over and above and against other faiths, especially Judaism, for centuries. We have imbibed the story of the Gospel too often as a version of, *We grasped what they failed to grasp*. We are taught that *we* are those who joined the faith that *they* rejected. But to do this—to see it in these oversimplified terms—is to misunderstand the Jewish context of Jesus's life, what Judaism is, when what we know as Judaism today really started, and how and when the early church was born and formed.

Jesus was Jewish, plain and simple. He wasn't just sort of Jewish, or temporarily Jewish. Jesus was born a Jew, and died a Jew. And every Christian who proclaims that Jesus was not just a figure in history, but was raised from the dead and lives today, needs also to realize that Jesus never once stepped foot in a church. Jesus was not even walking around Israel/Palestine when the word "Christian" was first used in the New Testament book of Acts nearly a generation after the death of St. Paul in Rome. (And Paul's death was about thirty years after Jesus's death and resurrection.) These are not the views of a conservative or a liberal; these are the facts as agreed upon by all Bible scholars.

In the book of Acts, we read about the early disciples of Jesus debating what it means to be Jewish and a follower of Jesus at the same time. This is because all the first followers of Jesus were Jewish, and after Jesus was gone from their midst they had to figure out what it meant to be a disciple of the rabbi. They were confused, and rightly so.

The most prominent of those early disciples, in terms of missionary activity, was St. Paul. About one-third of the New Testament was written by Paul. He was Jewish, we learn from his

writings (see Philippians 3:5), and then he became a follower of
Christ. He took his faith in Christ to the Gentiles—to non-Jews.
He had to figure out how to make the religious transition himself, and how to teach it to others. For example, did a follower
of Jesus not born Jewish have to become Jewish first, before
becoming Christian? Paul said no. There are many statements
about this in his letters in the New Testament—for example,
"But if you are led by the Spirit, you are not subject to the law"
(Galatians 5:18 NRSV). The other early disciples seem to have
agreed with him over time. But this was all new.

Any Christian quoting that verse of St. Paul, from Galatians
chapter 5, should do it carefully. It shouldn't be used ever as a
proof text (an isolated passage used to try and prove a proposition) for the irrelevance of Judaism, which did not exactly exist
when Paul said/wrote this. What we know today as Judaism
originated at about the same time as Christianity. What the
Hebrew Bible (or Old Testament) describes is ancient Israelite
religion involving priests, animal sacrifice, and a central Temple
in Jerusalem. This changed rapidly at about the same time the
first followers of Jesus began calling themselves "Christians."
The century of Jesus is the century of the birth of both Christianity and what we know today as Judaism (what Jews and Judaism call "Rabbinic Judaism"). And Judaism today bears almost
no resemblance to the faith and practices of the ancient Israelites. (For more on this, see chapter 1, "You Can't Understand
Judaism Simply Reading the Old Testament.")

A verse such as that one in Galatians 5 also should never be
said or quoted as if it is an end to a discussion or an argument
in apologetics of "our" faith vs. "their" faith. There is no evidence that Paul saw himself as ceasing to be Jewish. There was
no radical separation of two "faiths"—even the term "faith" is
of more recent origin (see Richard C. Lux's article, "Superses-
sionism/Replacement Theology," chapter 5). Jews who believed
that Jesus was the Messiah were part of a first-century Judaism under Roman rule that was diverse and fluid. At that time,
all Jews were equally persecuted minorities in ancient Rome,
whether they were Jews following what was being born as early

Judaism or whether they were Jews who were now starting to call themselves Christians.

All people of good will in the Roman Empire lamented the destruction of the Second Temple in 70 CE in Jerusalem, including Jews and Christians. This happened just a few years after St. Paul and St. Peter were martyred in Rome, and just after the Gospels of Matthew and Luke were written down. Anyone not worshiping the Roman gods was subject to persecution, including those who were beginning to center their faith on the life, ministry, and resurrected life of Jesus Christ. It was only after the destruction of the Temple in 70 that both the early Christian church and Rabbinic Judaism really began to take shape (see chapter 3 by Mary Boys). The last of the writings in the New Testament, for instance, can be reliably dated to around 100 CE, at least a generation after the deaths of St. Peter and St. Paul and the destruction of the Temple.

It was then only after Emperor Constantine made Christianity the safe and preferred religion of the empire, in 312 CE, that Judaism remained the religious tradition to be persecuted. Christians, then, many of them, took a "victory lap." What they should have done, then and since, is remember what it is like to suffer for their faith, rather than cause the suffering of others less fortunate.

So to start, we need to stop blaming, and hating, and killing our religious siblings. The Jewish people are our "elder siblings," as Pope John Paul II once said. This is historically and religiously true. Then, we need to go beyond not hating and not hurting and begin to see all the ways that we misuse and misappropriate Jewish texts, ritual, teachings, and tradition. For example, a Christian poet perhaps doesn't realize how inappropriate it is for her to write with Christian confidence, yet in the guise of a Hebrew psalmist or Hebrew prophet. She writes lines such as these, reflecting on Psalm 74 and its "O God, why hast thou cast us off forever?"

Come, Lord, O come with speed!
This sacrilegious seed

Root quickly out, and headlong cast;
All that thy holy place
Did late adorn and grace,
Their hateful hands have quite defaced.
            Poet Mary Herbert, 1561–1621

Prophets of the Hebrew Bible—*Jewish* prophets—may talk
this way, about themselves and their people, to call all back
to faithfulness. So the prophet Amos can channel God, saying:
"You only have I known of all the families of the earth; therefore I will punish you for all your iniquities" (Amos 3:2). But a
Christian does not get to talk this way about those same people,
who are—at least in this important regard—not her own. As
Christians, we should clean up our own house, first; that work
should keep us busy for a lifetime and more. And here we come
full circle with a reminder of why we need this book.

That God-wrestling psalmist's question is not answered
simply and only by the coming of Christ. There is another
covenant—the first and older one—which is unbroken and
unashamed. Jewish leaders like St. Paul were upset that their
coreligionists (other Jews) did not see Christ in glory, but they
also didn't think that everyone who was a Jew was destined to,
or necessarily needed to, become a Jesus-follower. It has taken
most of the rest of us two thousand years to learn this lesson.
And we still need to learn it.

PART ONE

Foundations

Chapter 1

You Can't Understand Judaism Simply Reading the Old Testament

Jon M. Sweeney

I was talking with a religion professor at a large university in the American South the other day. He's a friend of mine. He's a Christian. He teaches world religions to undergraduates. He said: "Most of my students, when they first enter my classroom, believe that the faith and practices of Jews today are what they have read about in the Old Testament in Sunday School."

Now I've heard this before, and I've met people—adults, with an interest in matters of faith—who also believe this. But on this day, I said to my friend, with my tongue somewhat in my cheek, "Don't they wonder where the priests are, and the animal sacrifice?"

He didn't miss a beat.

"They assume animal sacrifices are still going on," he said. He was serious. "That's part of why they think Jews and synagogues are scary."

I'm scared at how little we seem to know about each other in the twenty-first century.

* * *

The most fundamental misunderstanding of Christians toward Jews today throughout the world is the view held, unfortunately, by a majority of us in the pews who think that Judaism equals what we read in the Old Testament. This misunderstanding is both pervasive and dangerous.

The truth is, what we know as Judaism is only about as old as the Christian church. Judaism and Christianity are siblings. They both began about two thousand years ago. What we read about in the Old Testament—which we should, instead, refer to as the "Hebrew Bible," to avoid marking it as the "out-of-date" kind of "old"—describes the beginnings and activities and teachings of ancient Israel, a people. Those people went into exile (forced to leave what we call the Holy Land) during what is called the Babylonian Captivity[1] about six centuries before Christ. Nearly five centuries after they came back from this captivity, the Roman Empire came to rule Israel, and in the context of the Roman Empire both Judaism and Christianity were born.

You'll need to research these matters further, if you are seriously interested. There is much to read, much to know. You will find, for instance, that the Mishnah of Judaism was written roughly a century after the New Testament. Many themes in the Mishnah are similar to what one finds in the New Testament.

You will also find—and by this point in this book, you've read this before—that Jesus was a Jew and a rabbi. So when Jesus argues with the Pharisees, for instance, it isn't a case of two faiths debating but two rabbis debating. Think about it that way the next time you read in the Gospels where Jesus is correcting a Pharisee. Jesus was colleague and cousin with Pharisees; they were his fellow Jews and fellow teachers of Torah.

You will also find that much of what Jesus teaches comes from the Torah, the essential Scriptures for Jews and Judaism: what we sometimes call the Pentateuch, or the first five books of the Bible. Perhaps most importantly—because Christians are

---

1. In our day every term can be further researched in seconds, so we will not pretend to exhaust definitions, dates, and names of people. You can look these things up easily, and hopefully, you will read beyond what you discover here. You will also discover that the contributors to this book don't agree on all points. That is fine and good. One of our aims is to spark much necessary conversation in the church.

often taught that Christianity is about grace, and Judaism is about law—the commandment that Jesus said was "like unto" the first and greatest commandment (to love God with all your heart, mind, and spirit), "To love your neighbor as yourself," comes from the book of Leviticus. In the Torah.

CHAPTER 2

"Israel Is My Firstborn Son" (Exodus 4:22): The Statement of Yhwh regarding the Ancient Israelites

WALTER BRUEGGEMANN

This quite remarkable assertion by God occurs in the Exodus narrative when Moses is engaged in hotly contested negotiations with Pharaoh. Pharaoh is intent on keeping his supply of cheap labor in the form of enslaved Hebrews. He regards the Hebrews as nobodies without rights and without any ground from which to challenge his exploitative rule. In response to Pharaoh's obdurate policies, Moses is authorized by Yhwh, the promise-making God of Genesis, to insist on the emancipation of the Hebrew slaves. From the outset of the narrative we have known that Yhwh intends that emancipation. But now in 4:22 the ground for emancipation intensifies as Yhwh utters (beyond the divine promise of Exodus 3:7–9), a nonnegotiable reason for that emancipation. God has already called Israel "my people" (Exodus 3:7). Now, beyond that, God declares Israel to be "my firstborn son."

I

This imagery is unapologetically situated in a patriarchal system of primogeniture. In that system fathers had a peculiar commitment to their firstborn sons, a commitment voiced, for example, in the pathos of Esau and the helplessness of Isaac in Genesis 27. As a result of this social practice, the oldest son has specific expectations that match the obligation of the father.[1] The firstborn son is due to be heir to all that the father has. The primary gift of the father is to bless the son; that blessing from the father includes the family name, the family future, and the family property. Of course, the oldest son can receive none of these blessings if he remains enslaved, because slaves do not inherit property or anything else. As a result, the father is ada-mant and uncompromising about emancipation, which is the indispensable precondition of keeping the promise to which the father is committed. In the case of the Exodus narrative, the father has a promise of land to give to the son (Exodus 3:8), but the son cannot receive it as long as Pharaoh holds the son in slavery. Verse 23 adds an additional strong notice that puts the firstborn of Pharaoh in jeopardy; that divine threat is performed by God in the final exchange with Pharaoh (Exodus 12:29–32). The rhetoric of YHWH ups the ante even further:

> The firstborn of Pharaoh;
> The firstborn of the prisoner;
> The firstborn of the livestock. (12:29)

God is ready and able to intensify forceful action for the sake of God's oldest son. In desperate response, Pharaoh finally adheres to the counsel his advisors had given him long before (10:7). Pharaoh finally concedes the point at great cost to his regime and issues his decree of emancipation for Israel to Moses and Aaron:

> Rise up, go away from my people, you and the Israelites!
> Go, worship the Lord, as you have said. Take your flocks
> and your herds, as you have said, and be gone. And bring
> a blessing on me too! (12:31–32)

---

1. The exclusionary implications of the masculine rhetoric of patriarchy in the Bible are of course subject to acute critique. My purpose here, however, is otherwise, and I will seek to remain inside that imagery as best I can.

The father has invested a great deal in assuring the legacy of the firstborn son. This final utterance of Pharaoh not only permits Israel to go free, it recognizes that the force of divine blessing is only in the gift of the God of Israel. (It will be a long time before the prophet Isaiah voices God's blessing on Egypt, a fulfillment of Pharaoh's desperate petition [Isaiah 19:24–25].) It is this violent, uncompromising action by the father that begins the history of his firstborn son. Emancipated Israel abruptly enters history and is on its way to its "inheritance" at the behest of the father. This peculiar commitment by the father and this peculiar future by the son are further acknowledged in the divine utterance at Sinai:

> Indeed, the whole earth is mine, but you shall be for me a priestly kingdom and a holy nation. (Exodus 19:5–6)

Yнwн is creator and Lord of all; that claim, however, does not detract from the special promise given to the firstborn son and the special duty imposed on the firstborn son; Israel is on its way as God's distinctive covenant partner.

II

The imagery of God as father and Israel as firstborn son does not reappear often in the Hebrew Bible/Old Testament. We may consider three poignant uses of such imagery, all of which arise in moments of acute crisis when the future of Israel is at risk. First, more than any other text, Hosea 11:1–9 fully exploits the imagery of father–son and traces out the pathos-filled drama of that relationship. In verses 1–4, the father God reminisces about the early happy days of parenting, happy days that began with the wonder of the Exodus enacted by the father whereby the son was called out to covenantal life. God the father was end-lessly attentive to son Israel, teaching the child to walk, embracing him, healing him, and feeding him . . . all the caring acts that are remarkable for a father in patriarchal society.

From the outset, however, the son was recalcitrant, fleeing the call of the father, refusing the healing offered by the father.

In an angry reaction, the father is ready to deliver the son to the consequences of his own foolish, recalcitrant choices (vv. 5–7). But then, right in the midst of angry venting, the father stops short, "comes to himself," and reverses field (vv. 8–9). The father discovers, in this moment of rage, that his deep abiding love for his firstborn son overrides his anger. The father will not (cannot!) treat his eldest son as he has treated Sodom and Gomorrah (a.k.a. Admah and Zeboiim). In the end the father's commitment to the son prevails. The firstborn son continues, in spite of recalcitrance, to be the beloved heir of all that is in the gift of the father who will not act like an ordinary "mortal," that is, like an angry rejecting father.

Second, the same stunning drama of anger and embrace is lined out by Jeremiah. After the displacement of exile, Jeremiah poeticizes the internal life of God that leads to the restoration of Israel:

> I will lead them back,
> I will let them walk by brooks of water,
> in a straight path in which they shall not stumble;
> For I have become a father to Israel,
> and Ephraim is my firstborn. (Jeremiah 31:9)

The ground for restoration is the identity of Israel. Israel/Ephraim is God's firstborn, suggesting the father's unwavering commitment to the son. Then in 31:20 the poetry gives voice to the internal struggle in God's own heart:

> Is Ephraim my dear son?
> Is he the child I delight in?
> As often as I speak against him,
> I still remember him.
> Therefore I am deeply moved for him;
> I will surely have mercy on him, says the Lord.
>   (Jeremiah 31:20)

Yes, God does speak against Israel. God has been doing so through prophets and has good ground for such speech. But yes, Israel is nonetheless still the cherished son, the child of delight. The poetry has God own up to anger, but then to the recognition that cherishing Israel as firstborn son outlasts any anger. It is that awareness that leads God to the "therefore" that turns the poetry. God will indeed have mercy on his son, Israel. As with Hosea, Jeremiah sees that God's commitment to the son outruns rejecting anger and provides ground for restoration. This for Israel is the God who makes a way home out of no way!

Third, this awareness of the father that reached through anguish is matched in Isaiah 63:15–64:22 by Israel's pathos-filled lament. This lament is the plural voice of Israel in its displacement of exile or thereafter. But this lament could as well be the pathos-filled petition of Israel in any of its many seasons of anguish, including the brutality of the twentieth century. The lament begins with a reminder to God of what God seems to have forgotten or neglected:

> For you are our father,
> though Abraham does not know us and Israel does not
>   acknowledge us;
> you, O Lord, are our father;
> our Redeemer from of old is your name. (63:16)

The present generation of Israel that speaks here has been cut off from the promises. This is followed by a wonderment, "Why?," and then an imperative, "Turn back" (v. 17). The same note is reiterated in Isaiah 64. Again God is reminded of God's identity as Israel's father:

> Yet, O Lord, you are our father;
> we are the clay, and you are our potter. (v. 8)

The imagery of father is linked to that of "potter/clay," which asserts that Israel is wholly the outcome of the work of the father and is wholly dependent on the father. Then again comes the petition:

> Do not be exceedingly angry, O Lord,
> and do not remember iniquity forever.
> Now consider, we are all your people. (v. 9)

But the poem ends with searing wonderment:

> Will you restrain yourself, O Lord?
> Will you keep silent, and punish us severely? (v. 12)

Will God restrain the mercy for which Israel hopes? Will God remain silent and let brutality work its will against the firstborn son? The poem leaves the matter unresolved, as it has often been unsettled for Israel. The larger tradition invites us to see that the probes of verse 12 have been answered negatively: No, God will not restrain mercy. No, God will not keep silent. The evidence of historical experience, however, is not obvious or easy, given the vagaries of history and the brutalities of antisemitism.

In sum, the imagery of "firstborn son" turns up infrequently in the biblical tradition but at pivotal points. Israel holds a peculiar and preeminent place in the shape and intent of creation. This claim is wide and deep in Israel's normative narrative. We may believe, moreover, that it is also the way of YHWH who is fully and deeply embedded in Israel's poetic testimony.

III

When we stay inside the patriarchal imagery of primogeniture, to which Scripture attests (as I have sought to do here), we are left with unfinished wonderments.

1. The claim of the primacy and absolute entitlement of the firstborn son establishes Israel's special status with God. We must notice, however, that the traditional practice of primogeniture in Israel is dramatically subverted on two occasions. In Genesis 27:1–40 the second son, Jacob, by cunning and stealth, receives the blessing of father Isaac that properly belongs to firstborn Esau (see also 25:29–34). In Genesis 48:13–14 father Joseph enigmatically crosses his hands and gives to Ephraim (a stand-in for Israel) the blessing that rightly belongs to Manasseh, who is here identified as the firstborn. If the right of the firstborn son can be so readily reassigned, that social reality in the narrative seems to make the entitlement of the firstborn son less than absolute and sure.

2. The firstborn son, in all of Israel's narratives, is not the "only born." We may wonder then in what ways and to what extent the firstborn son must notice and pay attention to the reality of later-born siblings, who cannot be disregarded. Thus Israel as firstborn son is surrounded by siblings, notably heirs of Ishmael (Arabs) and, in contemporary time, specifically Palestinians. The firstborn son is drawn to the reality of the family and must, in some way treat these siblings responsibly as they share in the family legacy—just as those siblings must be responsible in their treatment of the firstborn.

3. The firstborn son of Yhwh lives in the real world of religious pluralism alongside the Christian claim of Jesus as "the only begotten son of God." As long as each tradition lives in a silo of isolation, each claim could remain unqualified. But there was never a time for such isolation. Only recently has there been positive energetic attention to the tension of these claims, a tension that requires irenic and thoughtful reflection, as for example in *Nostra Aetate,* from Vatican II, and *Dabru Emet,* by a company of Jewish scholars. It may be that the firstborn son Israel can acknowledge this belated "only begotten son" as a sibling; or it may be that the community of "the only begotten son" will come to terms with a firstborn sibling who has primary family entitlements. Such matters are not easy, but denial of that reality by either or both interpretive communities is like having an unwelcome and unexpected relative awkwardly show up at a reunion. Both claims (and both family members) are inescapably there.

4. In the context of Scripture there is no doubt that the recognition of Israel as firstborn son of Yhwh is a revelatory disclosure. It turns out, however, that that stunning revelatory disclosure, over time, in some circles has become an ideological tool of preference and privilege that serves exploitative self-interest (as in the case of West Bank "settlers"). I suggest that revelation becomes self-serving ideology whenever it becomes deeply linked to worldly power. So it has been for a long time in the church whenever the distinctive claims of Christian faith have been linked to worldly power; for the church that linkage has

led to abuse toward the Jewish people throughout the centuries. So it is that the revelatory claims of the Hebrew Bible pertain not only to Judaism but to worldly power linked to Judaism as well. It is the case that the biblical assertion of "firstborn son" is addressed to Israel in circumstances of acute vulnerability, first in Egyptian bondage (Exodus 4:22), and then amid the Babylonian exile (Jeremiah 31:9, 20). When that same revelation is heard in contexts of worldly power, it takes on a very different texture. Every religious tradition grounded in divine revelation must tread knowingly and self-critically in the face of the seductions of worldly power that distort reassuring disclosure into self-serving ideology. The revelatory claim of Israel as firstborn son of the father is not in doubt. That revelatory claim, however, continues to require thoughtful, faithful, critical parsing both by its adherents and by those of us who are elsewhere grounded.

Chapter 3

Christianity's Complicated Origins

Mary C. Boys, SNJM

Each week I look forward to a weekly column in the *New York Times*, "Metropolitan Diary," an often humorous and sometimes poignant set of anecdotes from readers about life in New York City. One of my favorites involves the 2009 romantic comedy *It's Complicated*, starring Meryl Streep and Alec Baldwin, submitted in February 2010 by Susan Kleinman:

> *Dear Diary:*
> Here's Abbott and Costello, as unwittingly performed by my husband and mother-in-law, who came to baby-sit last month:
> *Mother-in-law:* "You're going to a movie, then brunch?"
> *My husband:* "No, brunch then the movie—'It's Complicated.'"
> *She:* "Then do the movie first. What are you seeing?"
> *He:* "I just told you: 'It's Complicated.'"
> *She:* "What's so complicated? If you can't see the movie you want, I heard that new one with Meryl Streep is good. What's it called again?"

Most of us can remember a time when a conversation went awry, each party operating on a different wavelength. And the complexities of life regularly remind us that things are very complicated indeed, often in discomfiting ways. So, too, in the religious sphere. It can be tempting to hang on to ideas conveyed to us as children that we regarded as certainties, yet the crises and dilemmas inevitable in maturing often make us search for more adequate understandings.

"It's complicated" is particularly applicable to the history of Christian interactions with Jews and Judaism. Scholarship in the last fifty years about the relationship between the two traditions requires an "upgrade" to what we may have been taught or absorbed earlier in our lives. More recent insights enable us to reset the contentious conversations with Jews that characterized much of our common history.

In the following section, I present a sketch of Christian origins that typifies how many Christians understand the beginnings of their tradition in relation to Judaism. Some may explain this account in fuller detail and with varying emphases. But in my experience, this sketch provides the fundamental contours of understandings many Christians hold in common—if for no other reason than that no one has presented an alternative. The heart of this chapter, however, is an alternate account shaped by recent scholarship that serves as a corrective to flawed assumptions, insufficient data, and unreliable conclusions. It is this alternate perspective, I believe, that can provide us with fresh lenses on our Scriptures, a deepened sense of our own Christian identity, and new possibilities for engaging in a conversation with Jews. In a third section, I briefly explain key methodologies essential to this contemporary reading and point to ways this scholarship is embedded in my own Catholic Christianity.

A Typical Rendition of Christian Origins

Christianity fulfills the promises God made to Jews in the Old Covenant. The Jewish religion—Judaism—emphasized faithful adherence to the Law (Torah) as a way of life, but over time it became mired in legalism, exemplified by the Pharisees. Jesus's way of love, in contrast to the law of the Jews, threatened Jewish authorities. While technically the Roman governor of Judea, Pontius Pilate, authorized the crucifixion, it was the Jews who agitated for the death of Jesus. Although the New Testament depicts Jesus as a Jew from Nazareth of Galilee, the coming of the Holy Spirit at Pentecost fifty days after his death and resurrection meant the birth of Christianity. Thus, when we think of the first generations of the disciples of Jesus—including Peter, James, and Mary of Magdala—we think of them as Christians and the original members of the church, separate now from the synagogue. The apostle Paul, a convert from Judaism, helped to spread Christianity throughout the Mediterranean region, and it grew rapidly while Judaism declined.

A Perspective Grounded
in Contemporary Biblical Scholarship

We're so accustomed to speaking about Jews and Christians/ Judaism and Christianity that we overlook the layers of meaning in those terms as they developed over the two thousand years that our traditions have been in relationship. So it is important to sort out the evolution of these terms and to recognize the fluidity with which they were used in the formative period of both traditions. In other words, recognition of complicated Christian beginnings holds clues for new relationships with Jews in our time.

Originally, "Jew" meant a "Judean," a member of the people of Judea, and thus its layers were originally geographic and ethnic. During the period of the Maccabees (ca. 167–37 BCE), "Jew" came to include allies of the Judean state, a political community that transcended the physical boundaries of Judea. Over time another stratum emerged: a Jew was someone who believed in certain tenets (e.g., worship of the one God who made heaven and earth and gave Israel the Torah) and observed certain practices (e.g., Sabbath, circumcision, dietary and purity norms, sacrifices in the Temple in Jerusalem, and annual contribution of a half-shekel donation for its upkeep). In this usage, Judaism denoted a culture and a way of life distinct from "pagan" and "Greek" ways. And while holding in common these tenets and practices, Jews differed from one another in how they interpreted Torah, observed Shabbat, and followed the dietary laws. The significance of the Temple in Jerusalem varied in part depending on location, holding more importance for Jews in Judea than it did for those who lived farther away in the Galilee and even farther away in communities around the Mediterranean. Paula Fredriksen suggests that we will better understand the variant ways in which Judaism was lived "if we imagine the Torah as widely dispersed sheet music: the notes were the notes, but Jews played a lot of improv."[1] Among those playing "improv" were associations such as the Essenes, Pharisees, Sadducees, and Zealots. A later age would speak of them as voluntary groups formed around shared understandings and ways of practice.

In the initial phase of what eventually would become Christianity, in the late 20s and early 30s of the first century of the Common Era (CE) the Jewish teacher Jesus of Nazareth taught about God's kingdom through word and deed. Jesus's disciples were Jews who seemed to have limited interaction with Gentiles (non-Jews). These disciples also constituted a voluntary group. The New Testament sometimes speaks of them as "Followers of the Way" (Acts 9:2; 18:26; 19:9, 23; 22:4; 24:22). Contemporary scholars often refer to them as "Jesus's movement," that is, those who accompanied Jesus in making known the ways of God.

In 33 CE (or 30; the precise chronology is unclear) Pontius Pilate, in his role as the Roman Empire's governor of Judea, executed Jesus by crucifixion. Then "Jesus's movement" took a distinctive turn, as some among his disciples experienced him alive, proclaiming that God had raised Jesus from the dead. For his followers, the resurrection was *the* decisive event, leading to an outpouring of the Spirit of God upon the community. Now the teaching and preaching were not only about the imminent coming of God's kingdom but also about Jesus as God's divine agent or messiah ("Christ").

Two other related developments contributed to the reshaping

---

1. Paula Fredriksen, *When Christians Were Jews: The First Generation* (New Haven, CT: Yale University Press, 2018), 185.

of the Followers of the Way. First, Paul and his colleagues spread the word about Jesus to Gentiles throughout the Mediterranean region. As a closer reading of the New Testament reveals, Paul considered himself still an "Israelite," but one who had a call to preach the Way of Jesus to the Gentiles. While tradition has viewed Paul as a convert to "Christianity," a large body of contemporary scholarship offers a more nuanced understanding. Paul was a Jesus-following Jew called to make known the one God to Gentiles.[2]

Second, as a result of Paul's preaching, by the end of the first century of the Common Era, the Followers of the Way included large numbers of Gentiles. Their inclusion intensified questions about identity, including to what extent non-Jewish followers of Jesus should follow Jewish practices such as the dietary laws, circumcision for men, and observance of Sabbath. For the early communities, controversies over such matters of practice took precedence over later theological questions such as Jesus's divine-human status, which preoccupied church leaders of the fourth and fifth centuries.

It was during the 70s to the early 100s of the second century CE that rivalry between the other Jewish groups and the Followers of the Way (now a mixed Jewish/Gentile group) increased. They debated about whose was the more faithful way to God: The Way of Torah or the Way of Jesus? Because this was also the time frame for the composition of the four Gospels, some of the tensions of their debate were reflected in certain Gospel passages such as the diatribe against the Pharisees in Matthew 23 and John's frequent identification of "the Jews" as Jesus's principal opponents. That is, the Gospel writers integrated the disputes of their time into their narratives of the ministry of Jesus; the disputes of the late-first and early-second centuries CE found their way into depictions of what Jesus said and did. The heightened language in these texts reflects characteristic rhetorical conventions of antiquity in which denunciation of

---

2. See Krister Stendahl, *Paul among Jews and Gentiles* (Philadelphia: Fortress Press, 1976). Stendahl first proposed this view of Paul in a lecture in 1963.

the other was an art form. What later generations failed to recognize, however, is that these were intrafamilial arguments, not those of "Christian" pitted against "Jew."

The first three centuries of the Common Era were the womb out of which both Judaism and Christianity emerged; the back-and-forth conversations and arguments helped to shape each. We can point neither to a specific issue nor to a specific time when the two traditions regarded themselves as separate religions, although the Council of Nicaea in 325 may be one of the key indices of a clearer parting at the level of the official leadership of the church. The people, however, seemed to exhibit a more fluid identity. In late-fourth-century Antioch, for example, John Chrysostom assailed his congregants who were also attracted to Jewish festivals and practice of Jewish customs, attacking them as "Judaizers" who were "sick with Judaism."

By this point, the church's leaders no longer saw an intrafamilial argument, as was the case in New Testament writings, but rather that of binary opposites: Jesus versus the Jews, church versus the synagogue.[3] From this binary a tragic history ensued. Biblical scholarship of our time allows us a reset so that what had become a point of division can be restored to a conversation about not simply our differences but our common call to heal the world.

Contemporary Biblical Scholarship and the Christian Churches

As readers of this chapter are undoubtedly aware, "Christianity" is an enormous umbrella, covering significant differences in matters of biblical interpretation, theology, ritual, practice, and relation to other religions and the larger culture. My own standpoint is that of a practicing Catholic with extensive experience in ecumenical and interreligious work, principally Jewish–Christian relations. I hold in common with many Protestant

---

3. See Amy-Jill Levine, *The Misunderstood Jew: The Church and the Scandal of the Jewish Jesus* (New York: Harper One, 2007).

colleagues the contemporary biblical scholarship I draw on in this essay, as well as that of Jewish scholars of the New Testament. One of the great gifts of our time is the way in which diverse scholars of Bible collaborate, including lively discussion of variations in method and conclusions.

In contrast, scholars and pastors from fundamentalist churches work from dramatically different premises, and thus reach starkly distinctive conclusions. My intent here is not to argue with fundamentalist readings but simply to make clear that the contemporary biblical scholarship crucial to my understanding of Christian origins is not universally accepted. So I wish to make explicit a few of the ground rules that constitute contemporary biblical scholarship and then to situate these methods in my own ecclesial tradition.

Perhaps the most important principle is that biblical texts must be understood in their literary, social, and historical contexts. Since the biblical authors do not explain their contexts, a considerable amount of analysis is required—a vast army of linguists, archaeologists, historians, religious thinkers, and social scientists contributes to the interpretation of biblical texts. In terms of the New Testament, scholars regard the written Gospels as originating ca. 70s–110 CE; in this perspective, the genre "gospel" does not accord with our modern sense of a historically reliable account but rather means something akin to a testimonial, a bearing witness by the second and third generations of followers of Jesus. Further, scholars see the Gospels as emanating from specific communities of believers who themselves were grappling with the issues of their day in light of the teaching of Jesus as had been passed down to them in the oral tradition.

For example, what Matthew's community was experiencing in the mid-80s of the first century shaped the crafting of his narratives; since Matthew did not provide an explanation of his context, scholars infer from the emphases of his Gospel. One case in point: Matthew's Gospel has considerable material about conflict and forgiveness within a community (e.g., chapter 18); it seems reasonable to conclude his community was wrestling with conflicts within their own group, looking to Jesus's parables, prayer, and deeds for guidance. Another case in point: John's Gospel frequently speaks of "the Jews," most often portraying them in negative fashion. Despite energetic efforts to uncover the precise reasons for his depiction, scholars tentatively conclude that his community had serious disagreements with a particular group of Jews; by the terminology "the Jew," John was not characterizing the Jews but rather those whom his community opposed.

I emphasize that this scholarship exists within the life of many church traditions today. Thus, I want to add a very brief word about biblical scholarship within the context of Catholic teaching; the dialogue between scholars and church leaders has become a vital dimension of Catholic–Jewish relations. The most significant stimulus for renewed appreciation of Scripture comes from the Second Vatican Council (1962–1965), including the imperative from *Dei Verbum* §22: "Access to sacred scripture ought to be widely available to the Christian faithful." Another of the council's decrees, *Nostra Aetate,* ignited study, reflection, and dialogue with Jews in formal and informal ways. Its insistence that the death of Jesus "cannot be charged against all Jews, without distinction, then alive, nor against Jews today" (§4) would be deepened in statements by the Commission on Religious Relations with the Jews and by study documents from the Pontifical Biblical Commission, especially the latter's *The Jewish People and Their Sacred Scriptures* in 2001. Two teaching documents from the United States Conference of Bishops, though issued in 1988, remain readable and relevant: *God's Mercy Endures Forever* and *Criteria for the Evaluation of the Dramatizations of the Passion.* All these documents are readily available on various websites. Catholics who wish to see biblical commentaries representative of their tradition might do well to consult the various editions of *The Jerome Biblical Commentary,* originally published in 1968, revised in 1989; *The Jerome Biblical Commentary: Fully Revised Edition* will soon be forthcoming.

Healthy religious traditions renew themselves after crises. For example, after the fall of the Temple in Jerusalem in 70 CE and the subsequent destruction of that city, many surviving Jews moved into the Galilee, pondering what it meant that their central sacred space no longer existed. Torah then came to function as a "portable Temple," and Shabbat as the sanctification of time rather than, as in the Temple, a sanctification of space.

So, too, for Christians. In the wake of the Second World War and the Holocaust, some Christians began to realize how much their long and, at times, violent argument with Judaism had brought tragedy to the Jewish people and shame to the church. For Catholics, the recognition of a responsibility to reset relations grew out of the renewal Vatican II initiated in the church. Of particular significance is the recognition that our origins in Jewish life were far more complicated than we had recognized. Acknowledging "it's complicated" has allowed a conversation that went grievously awry centuries ago to regenerate new possibilities for partnership in proclaiming God's desire for a world in which a just peace flourishes.

CHAPTER 4

The New Testament Was Written Entirely by Jews

NICHOLAS KING, SJ

Yet another shooting in a synagogue has reminded us all, Jews and Christians, that antisemitism and the politics of hatred are not yet dead. Our task in response to this is to recognize what terrible things Christians have done, or permitted to be done in our name, all down the centuries, culminating in the appalling barbarism of the Holocaust. The Catholic Church made a definitive response in the Second Vatican Council in the shape of the very important document *Nostra Aetate*, which makes it clear that the church "deplores all hatreds, persecutions, displays of antisemitism levelled at any time or from any source against the Jews," arguing that she "cannot forget that she received the revelation of the Old Testament by way of that people with whom God in his inexpressible mercy established the ancient covenant." For Catholic Christians, there can be no justification for antisemitism.

Scholarship has moreover moved on greatly since then and reminds us what we should never have forgotten, that Jesus was a Jew and so was his mother and so were all his first followers. So too, I might add, were all the authors of the New Testament. Paul, as we too easily forget, was a Jew; and some scholars argue that he might very well have had his son circumcised. None of the New Testament authors looked anywhere else but at the Old Testament to arrive at their understanding of the life and sayings of Jesus. Some people, be it noted, resist speaking of the "Old Testament" on the grounds that it is neither "Old" nor a "Last Will and Testament," and prefer to refer to it as the "First Testament" or the "Hebrew Scriptures." I shall be using the more familiar "Old Testament"; this in no way implies that it is somehow inferior, still less "superseded."

Paul the Jew

Paul, whom we first get to know as Saul, was unmistakably a Jew; he writes in Greek, but he was clearly at home in Hebrew and Aramaic; he argues by way of constant quotations from the Old Testament, even in his two surviving letters to the Corinthians, who were on the whole a Gentile audience; and his views on sexual morality come (admirably) from the Jewish tradition. It is true, of course, that he persecuted the infant Christian movement. He says so himself. And it is worth asking why he did so. My suggestion to you is that there were two reasons, both very Jewish. The first was that in Deuteronomy 21:22–23 it says that "God's curse hangs on him who hangs on a tree"; he alludes to that text in Galatians 3:13, and it is fair to presume that he cited it against the nascent Jesus movement. The second reason is that these Christians started very quickly to apply to Jesus language that hitherto had been reserved to God. A good Jew cannot run around saying that human beings are gods; that is what pagans do. But quite soon the early Christians realized that they could not do justice to their experience of Jesus without using such language.

So it was that when Paul met Jesus, he was in no doubt at all that he had done so; immediately he fell in love with Jesus and realized that if Jesus was no longer dead, then he was indeed part of God's story, because God had raised him from the "curse." Not only that, but if God had raised Jesus from the dead, then Jesus was indeed God's Messiah (as the Christians had been proclaiming—that is what the name "Christian" means). Reading the letters of Paul in the presumed order of their composition, it is possible to see Paul feeling his way toward a fitting language about Jesus, language that placed Jesus very close indeed to God. It is true, of course, that this led some of Paul's fellow-Jews to reject him, and even try to kill him. But Paul's profoundest attitude to his coreligionists is apparent in Romans 9–11, where Paul unfolds his sense of the centrality of Judaism in God's plan.

Mark's Gospel: Unmistakably Jewish

Mark invented the Gospel form, and this short text cannot be anything but Jewish. It starts with a quotation ostensibly from Isaiah (although in fact the first bit of poetry comes not from Isaiah but from Exodus or Malachi). And Mark's Christology reflects his Jewish roots; you can feel his hesitation about directly identifying Jesus as "God." Instead he indicates how Jesus does the kind of things that God does. Look, for example, at the forgiving of sins in the healing of the man on the stretcher in 2:1–12, or the awestruck question of the disciples after the calming of the storm: "Who is this, then, that even the wind and the sea obey him?" Good Jew as he is, Mark cannot give a direct answer to this question, and instead allows the readers to draw their own conclusion. There is nothing in all this that cannot be grasped from within the basic framework of religious Judaism. Indeed, it is not out of the question that the author of this Gospel was related to Paul and Barnabas, and there is an ancient legend that he was amanuensis to the undoubtedly Jewish Simon Peter.

Matthew: Jesus as the Fulfillment of Judaism

What about Matthew? He starts his version (which in large part depends on that of Mark) with his genealogy of Jesus. This gives the reader the Jewish lens through which to read the Gospel as a whole, tracing Jesus's ancestry back to Abraham, to whom God's promises were first delivered, then to David, under

whom they seemed to be fulfilled, to the exile in Babylon, when
many Jews thought that God had forgotten them, and finally
to the birth of Jesus, which Matthew presents as the climax of
Jewish history. Another addition by Matthew is that of the Sermon on the Mount (chapters 5–7). This is a very Jewish composition. Right at the center of this, and giving it structure, comes
the Lord's Prayer, which any Jew could recite without a blush,
except for the unfortunate fact that it is widely understood as a
"Christian invention." And what of Matthew's Christology? He
does it very delicately, for Matthew is a good Jew and knows
that this is a tricky area; but the reader might like to read, in
1:23, the verse in which Isaiah 7:14 is quoted, with the line "they
shall call him Emmanuel" (which Matthew kindly translates as
"God *with us*"). Then, at the very end of the Gospel (28:20), we
find Jesus's parting words, "I am *with you* always," and may
note the significance of this subtle echo. Another Jewish trait
that we find in Matthew is that of a proper caution about using
the name of "God" (Jewish writers in English will often spell
it "G-d"). Matthew often (but alas not always—scholars speak
of "redactional fatigue"!) changes Mark's "kingdom of God" to
"kingdom of heaven/the heavens."

Why, then, is Matthew sometimes regarded as the "most
anti-Jewish" of the Gospels? The evidence for this perception
is found in the very sharp, almost brutal chapter 23 (which you
should read only if you are feeling strong), with its sevenfold
repetition of "woe to you, scribes and Pharisees." The language
here is alarmingly polemic; it probably owes something to what
is nowadays called the "parting of the ways" between Matthew's church and the "synagogue across the road." Christians
down the centuries have admittedly used it for pouring whole-
sale obloquy on our Jewish brothers and sisters; but they have
missed the point. What we have here is not an attack on Jews as
such but the familiar tones of religious sibling rivalry, one Jewish group assailing another. There is an interesting and nearly
contemporary parallel to this sort of language in the community that produced the Dead Sea Scrolls. They speak of one or

more fellow Jews as the "Wicked Priest," "Seekers after Smooth Things," and "Men of the Lie." But it would be absurd to think of them as antisemitic. (Recently I heard a rabbi from one of England's biggest cities explaining why there were so many synagogues in the town: "You see, we Jews are always falling out with each other," he said). So what Matthew says in chapter 23 does not make him antisemitic.

John's Gospel and the "Jews"

What about the Gospel of John, then? It is a thoroughly Jewish Gospel from beginning to end, and not, as used sometimes to be argued, a "Hellenistic" production. But there is a major problem in that the Greek word *Ioudaioi*, which is standardly translated as "Jews," is frequently used for Jesus's opponents, who are arguing with him and planning to kill him and refusing to accept him (this issue is considered in greater detail elsewhere in this book). The usage sounds offensive in places, if you are sensitive to the threat of antisemitism; and I was talking recently to a woman who sings in choirs and who confided how difficult she had found it this year to sing Bach's *Passion according to John*, with its many references to "Jews." When it is sung in German, of course, with all the resonances that language has had since the Holocaust, the problem is even more acute; for "the Jews"/ *die Juden* always seem to be behaving badly in those chapters of the Gospel. One solution, which I adopted in my own translation of the Bible, was to translate the word invariably as "the Judeans," and many people have spoken of their relief at being thereby spared all those negative references to "the Jews." Like most solutions, this one does not always work, since there are times when *Ioudaioi* in John's Gospel clearly means not "inhabitants of the southern kingdom of Judea" but Jews; but in my judgment this is a price worth paying. I am certain, at all events, that the author of this remarkable piece of writing would be horrified at the notion that his Gospel might be used as grounds for killing or persecuting his coreligionists.

Ah! But What about Luke?

What then about the Gospel of Luke and its second volume, what we call the Acts of the Apostles? It is often stated as a matter of fact (though without any evidence) that Luke is a Gentile. I have no idea why this might be thought to be the case, except that there is a reference at Colossians 4:14 to Luke the doctor. Presumably it is assumed—illogically—that if this person is the author of the Third Gospel and of its second volume, and if he was a doctor, then he must have been a Gentile. Alternatively, the argument might be that our author writes excellent Greek, in various different styles, and shows little acquaintance with Hebrew. But it is quasi-racist ignorance to suggest that a Jew cannot write good Greek, and indeed there are many Jews whose Hebrew is limited, but who write, for example, beautiful English. Furthermore, this author is entirely at home in the Old Testament in its Greek version, which we call the Septuagint; and he begins and ends his story in the Temple at Jerusalem, which functions almost as a character in his narrative. Likewise, it is only Luke who has Jesus deliver four sad "oracles" over Jerusalem; and in his second volume there is constant dialogue between the representatives of the Jesus movement and the Jewish authorities. The final example of these is in the very last chapter of Acts. It is true that these encounters are often tense or confrontational, with imprisonment and flogging and killing, and at times a kind of despair that the Jewish people were not responding to the gospel as Gentiles were doing. But that is inner-religious debate, which, as in the case of Matthew above, is often especially heated. It does not follow from that, however, that the author of Luke–Acts is encouraging his readers to hate Jews, still less to kill them, and the author would be astonished at such a conclusion. Some of the loveliest parables of Jesus are found in Luke's Gospel. The stories of the Good Samaritan or the Prodigal Son presume a Jewish background. For these reasons, Luke is certainly best understood as a Jewish author from an urban Greek background who is at home in one or other of the big cities of the Eastern Mediterranean.

Conclusion

There is no space here to afford this same treatment to the rest of the New Testament. I have argued that the New Testament is best understood as the work of Jewish authors: I could offer you a similar account of the rest of the documents of our New Testament. The Letter to the Hebrews is deeply at home in Jewish religion and writings; the Letter of James is sometimes thought to be a "synagogue homily," and 1 and 2 Peter belong in a Jewish setting, admittedly in the Hellenistic world. The three letters of John, though they are not all the same sort of thing, belong in the same world as the Fourth Gospel; and the Letter of Jude comes from the same Jewish background, and indeed quotes the very Jewish document that we know as *Enoch*.

There remains only that extraordinary work with which the Christian Bible ends, what we call the Apocalypse, or Revelation. In this work there are, in the view of many scholars, more references to or citations from the Old Testament than there are verses. The Greek in which the book is written sounds much more like the kind of Greek that would be penned by someone brought up with Aramaic or Hebrew as their first language than what comes from the stylus of the author of Luke–Acts, so it is implausible to see this extraordinary vision as antisemitic. It is true that in 2:9 there is a reference to the "synagogue of Satan" and a clear reference at 11:8 to Jerusalem, "where their Lord was crucified," as "being called spiritually 'Sodom and Egypt.'" This is hardly polite, of course. It is not, however, the language of antisemitism, but, in both cases, of inner-Jewish polemic.

In short, I conclude that every word of the twenty-seven documents that this extraordinary library that is the New Testament contains was written by good Jews, and that it is unfounded, even perverse, to call it anti-Jewish. We must however confess, to our shame, that Christians, as well as Jews, have often read the New Testament in this way, with catastrophic results. No religion that peddles hatred and killing can be of God.

Chapter 5

Supersessionism/ Replacement Theology

Richard C. Lux

Supersessionism, sometimes called "replacement theology," is the doctrine that claims that Christianity and/or the Catholic Church has superseded or replaced the Jewish people as God's covenant people. It asserts that the "old" covenant that God had with Israel has been replaced by the "new" covenant in Jesus, and that Jews are no longer God's chosen people and are rejected by God. Only conversion to Christianity via Baptism can fully restore them to God's love and acceptance.

The French Jewish historian and Holocaust survivor Jules Isaac sketched out this Christian theological anti-Judaism that had been an integral part of Christian teaching since it began in the second century, reached its full maturation in the early Middle Ages, and continued until its complete rejection by the Second Vatican Council in its document *Nostra Aetate* ("In Our Age," 1965). In Isaac's book, *The Teaching of Contempt* (1962), he details this teaching of contempt in ten main themes, explaining how it:

1. Promulgates an erroneous, univocal, and stereotypical view of the religious and ethical world of the Hebrew Scriptures (the Old Testament).
2. Denies the indebtedness of Christianity to the religious genius of Judaism.

3. Denigrates first-century Palestinian Judaism.
4. Teaches that the dispersion of the Jews from the land of Israel was a divine punishment for their rejection of Jesus.
5. Fails to educate Christian people about the polemical (and intra-Jewish) character of certain texts of the Christian Scriptures (the New Testament), including the pejorative invoking of "the Jews" and caricatures of the Pharisees.
6. Characterizes Jesus in ways that reject his Jewishness and his fidelity to his Jewish tradition.
7. Conveys the erroneous impression of universal antipathy toward Jesus by Jews of his time, when in actuality only a small number of Jews—mainly the Temple priesthood—opposed Jesus.
8. Employs a singular, messianic interpretation of the religious motives of the Jews of Jesus's time (that is, that only a messianic expectation was prominent in the religious imaginations of the people and that only one particular understanding of messianism prevailed in Jewish belief).
9. Stereotypes Jewish leadership, and exonerates the Roman officials in the death of Jesus.
10. Charges the Jews with deicide, a charge "murderous . . . ," as Isaac wrote, "in its generation of hatred and crime but also . . . radically false."

History of the Development of Supersessionism

All the controversial passages in the Christian Scriptures regarding Jews, which were an in-house family argument within the Jewish community, were misunderstood in Christian understanding by the early second century, when the majority of Jesus's followers were then converted Gentiles with little or no knowledge of Jewish religion, culture, and history. In addition, the destruction of the Temple in Jerusalem in 70 CE brought about a profound change in Jewish belief and practice. The preaching and evangelism of the apostle Paul, his collaborators, and followers brought about the establishment of many Christian communities around the Mediterranean which were

Greek-speaking and almost entirely composed of formerly pagan Gentiles.

In this context, Marcion, a non-Jew, born in Pontus on the Black Sea, who came from a high social class and was well-educated, arrived in Rome about the year 140 CE. He was accepted into the Christian community there and began teaching. His dominant theme was that of the discontinuity between the Law, that is, the Torah, and the Gospel story concerning Jesus. He taught that the Old Testament was not fulfilled by, but abolished by, Jesus. The God of the Jews, according to Marcion, was a god without mercy who was vengeful, who severely punished, and who was in no way related to the God of Jesus, whose father was a God of love, forgiveness, and salvation. Even though Marcion was excommunicated and banished from the Christian community at Rome, he established his own church with bishops, priests, and deacons. His teaching and community spread throughout the Mediterranean, and its theology continues in some forms up to the present day. For even today in the church we sometimes hear preachers speak erroneously of the God of vengeance and punishment in the Old Testament, while Jesus's God in the New Testament is one of love and forgiveness.

Prior to the fourth century and the establishment of Christianity as the official religion in the Roman Empire by Constantine, anti-Judaic literature focused on the validity of the messiahship of Christ, the abolition of the Law, and the identity of the church as the replacement of Israel in the eyes of God. Noteworthy proponents of these positions were St. Justin Martyr (100–165), Tertullian (160–220), St. Hippolytus (170–236), and Origen (185–254), who said that the Jews' rejection of Jesus has resulted in their present calamity and exile. Origen also said that because of their crime against the Christ the Jews would never return to the Land of Israel, nor ever have a nation again.

By the end of the fourth century, when paganism died out and the early Christian heresies were overcome, the church looked on Judaism as the principal threat to the faith. The historian Eusebius of Caesarea (260–340) made the distinction between "Hebrews" and "Jews." The Hebrews were considered primitive Christians, noble and good, whereas "the Jews" were the despicable people living among us with their synagogues and religious practices.

The most venomous attack on the Jews was waged by St. John Chrysostom of Antioch (344–407) in his sermons. He called them murderers, people possessed by the devil, murderers of their own offspring whom they immolated to the devil. Their synagogues were houses of prostitution and the domicile of the devil as were the souls of the Jews! Chrysostom said that the Jews were degenerate because of their odious assassination of Christ. For this deicide, he said that there was no expiation possible, no pardon, and that vengeance is without end. Thus it was the duty of Christians to hate the Jews.

So not only had Christianity and the church superseded and replaced the Jewish people, but in the teaching and practice of the church a generalized popular hatred of the Jews was under way and would continue in Christianity well into the twentieth century.

While this teaching and preaching created an ill climate between Christian and Jews, it was the translation of this theology into legislation by the church and the empire that had the most devastating effect on the Jewish community.

The long history of anti-Judaism encompasses oppressive legislation directed at the Jews, including their status as members of the empire and their religious practices. By 450 CE the struggle with the church was lost, and although Judaism remained a licit religion in the empire, its practices, with its Jewish population, began to be more circumscribed and restricted.

Catastrophic events in later Jewish history growing out of these prejudices included the slaughter of Jews in their towns in the eleventh and twelfth centuries by Crusaders traveling on their way to the Holy Land to fight the Muslims. Also in the twelfth century, Jews were charged with "ritual murder," that is, the murder of a Christian, preferably a child, during Holy Week for Jewish religious practices—utterly false and salacious charges, which continued in Europe and even in the United States up to the twentieth century.

The Fourth Lateran Council, in 1215 CE, enacted further restrictions on the Jews, including confinement to a Jewish Quarter in towns and cities and the wearing of distinctive dress that identified them as Jews—a harbinger of Nazi Germany and the wearing of the Jewish star. The Black Death (the Plague) of 1347–1350 brought destruction and torture to Jewish communities all across Europe since Jews were accused of causing this plague. The Spanish Inquisition of the fifteenth century resulted in the expulsion (under pain of death unless baptized) for 300,000 Spanish Jews.

The antisemitism arising in the nineteenth century was racial, though ultimately rooted in supersessionist ideology, and it brought about the religious rejection of the Jews, which gradually began to spill over into nationalistic political ideology, resulting gradually in government-mandated prejudice and discrimination, in action and legislation. Becoming progressively more menacing, restrictive, and finally deadly, this antisemitism aimed at totally annihilating the Jewish people. The nadir was reached in Germany with Nazism (1933–1945), but the antisemitic behavior was imitated and supported by many Christians in the countries of Europe at the time of World War II.

The Christian rejectionist teaching of nineteen centuries was finally overturned by the Second Vatican Council in Rome on October 28, 1965, in the "Declaration on the Relation of the Church to Non-Christian Religions," called *Nostra Aetate* ("In Our Age"). In this document, the church recognizes "the spiritual ties that link the people of the New Covenant to the stock of Abraham." It echoes the teaching of the apostle Paul about "his kinsmen": "They are Israelites; theirs the adoption, the glory, the covenants, the giving of the law, the worship, and the promises, theirs the patriarchs, and from them, according to the flesh, is the Messiah" (Romans 9:4–5). St. Paul says that God does not take back the gifts he has bestowed (that is, the covenants) nor the choice that God made (Jews as the chosen people of God) (Romans 11:28–29). The church once and for all rejected the charge of deicide against the Jewish people by saying that "the Jews should not be spoken of as rejected or accursed as if this followed from holy Scripture." The Church also "reproves every form of persecution [and] . . . deplores all hatreds, persecutions, displays of antisemitism leveled at any time or from any source against the Jews."

The church now encourages dialogue with the Jews and has issued many documents in the fifty years since *Nostra Aetate* concerning how to continue to build positive relations with the Jewish people. And in 1993 the church (as Vatican City State) officially recognized the State of Israel and established diplomatic relations with it.

PART TWO

Progress

Chapter 6

Spiritual Practices on Ash Wednesday

Jon M. Sweeney

Ash Wednesday is, of course, the beginning of the season of Lent and a time for serious introspection. This is the time, most of all in the Christian year, when we focus ourselves on repentance for what has passed, and try to begin again at trying to live the gospel in the world. With that in my mind, at Mass each year on Ash Wednesday that familiar passage from the Gospel of Matthew, chapter 6, is read aloud.

"Jesus said to his disciples," it begins, and goes on to say, in summary: Go and perform good deeds, and repent of your sins. Oh, and don't do it like the hypocrites.

Here's the problem: The identity of those "hypocrites" is almost certainly misunderstood by many who hear it read aloud. How many Christians leave church with ashes on their foreheads on Ash Wednesday proud not to be like the hypocrites in the synagogues?

In Matthew 6, Jesus says: "Take care not to perform righteous deeds in order that people may see them. . . . When you give alms, do not blow a trumpet before you, as the hypocrites do in the synagogues and in the streets to win the praise of others."

Then later, Jesus says again: "When you pray, do not be like the hypocrites, who love to stand and pray in the synagogues and on street corners so that others may see them." So all of those hypocrites are in synagogues, far from where Jesus might be worshiping on a day like this. Right? You could easily think so, without historical understanding and context.

How many Christians leave Mass—or for non-Catholic liturgical Christians, leave a service where ashes are put on their foreheads—misunderstanding the meaning of Jesus's teaching? They may walk home on Ash Wednesday, to the subway, to their cars, off to work or shopping or whatever, thinking that as long as they are not like those hypocritical other people—perhaps the ones "in the synagogues"—they are OK before God.

Here's the worst part: Perhaps they pass by a synagogue as they are leaving church. One year, when I was living in Brooklyn during Lent, I remember passing three synagogues on my walk back to our apartment after the Ash Wednesday service. I wondered, as I was walking, how many Christians were thinking to themselves, seeing the entrance to one of those synagogues, "Those Jews, they are so unlike Jesus, and so different from how Jesus asked me to be." That would be to completely misunderstand the message of the gospel.

As you've read more than once by now, Jesus was a Jew. Jesus was a rabbi. In fact, he was talking only to his fellow religionists, to other Jews, when he said those words. This means that the correct interpretation today for the twice-repeated phrase, "as the hypocrites do in the synagogues," would be something more like, "as the hypocrites do in the churches." The hypocrites are us.

Many people today are energized by the explosion of information about the Jewishness of Jesus. We've come to understand more about this aspect of Jesus in the last 150 years than Christians grasped for the 1,850 years prior to that. These resources are changing how Christians and Jews relate to each other, and how Christians understand the origins of their faith. One immense, recent, insightful book is *The Jewish Annotated New Testament*, which I have read in local book groups, and which thousands of Christians and Jews (I've been in groups that include both) are using to discover the context in which Christianity was born. I recommend it to you.[1]

---

1. *The Jewish Annotated New Testament,* ed. Amy-Jill Levine and Marc Zvi Brettler, 2nd ed. (New York: Oxford University Press, 2017).

If we are going to use Jesus's teachings, during Lent or at any other time, I hope our "take away" focuses on the way these teachings show us how to be good twenty-first-century Christians, not about how to avoid being bad first-century Jews.

We have to learn to read our Scriptures with historical understanding. (See chapter 4, and read Nicholas King's discussion of how the author of Matthew was Jewish, and was arguing with other Jewish understandings of Jesus, in the Gospel of Matthew.) A historical understanding of the now-offensive phrase "in the synagogues" involves grasping the intra-Jewish fighting that was going on when Matthew's Gospel was first written.

We also need to read our Scriptures in ways that are always applying them to our lives, rather than the lives of others. This is fundamental to reading the gospel correctly. Scripture should never be a condemnation of someone else. Hearing the reading of "hypocrites . . . in the synagogues" for our lives would mean substituting the word "churches" for "synagogues"—because we aren't hearing the reading while standing in synagogue. To make that substitution, at least in our minds, on Ash Wednesday, would be to faithfully understand what the Scripture is saying to us on that day. Surely there are hypocrites in the churches, and surely that's what the Scripture means for our lives.

Lectio divina, or "divine reading," is one spiritual practice we might use to "enter into" the Scripture passage in a new way. It goes back to early monasticism when monks would not just study Scripture but treat it as a "living Word" for their lives. To practice *lectio,* we don't just read the passage but pause and meditate and pray with it, seeking to "enter into" it. Imagine yourself as one hearing the words of Jesus as he said those words for the very first time. Pope Benedict XVI said: "I . . . recommend the ancient tradition of *Lectio Divina*: the diligent reading of Sacred Scripture accompanied by prayer brings about that intimate dialogue in which the person reading hears God who is speaking, and in praying, responds to him with trusting openness of heart."[2]

---

2. Pope Benedict XVI, in 2005, on the fortieth anniversary of the Vatican II document *Dei verbum.*

Applying the living Word to your life is the ideal. I also know pastors have taken steps to help apply the meaning of the Ash Wednesday reading to the lives of their congregants through interpretation, discussion, and in a homily. In some churches, in fact, the word "churches" is actually substituted for "synagogues" in the reading, to avoid mistaken assumptions and to make easier the application.

* * *

Then there's the issue of what to do with the ashes on our foreheads when we leave church. "I proudly wear them to the office," one friend says to me. "To wipe them off would be like denying Christ," says another. The priest usually says to us as those ashes are applied: "Remember, you are dust and to dust you will return." That's the point—we are being reminded, tangibly as well as intellectually, of this truth. So taking those ashes with you down the street, to the store, to the office, seems like a good and necessary thing. I understand how you feel. I used to feel that way too. But then I changed my mind.

First of all, what did Jesus say about the hypocrites and how they pray? His point was not to show off, not to make your piety something you demonstrate to the people around you, as if you are winning heavenly points for it. It's kind of tough not to see a cross symbol of ashes on the forehead in that light.

And second, with many Jewish friends, and conscious as I am of how the cross symbol has been mistakenly and evilly used to abuse them and other non-Christians for centuries, I now realize that I'm not going to wear a cross on my forehead on this day, or any other day. I don't think that, for a moment, this dampens the fervency of my prayer on Ash Wednesday:

Father, our source of life, you know our [my] weakness. May we [I] reach out with joy to grasp your hand and to walk more readily in your ways. We [I] ask this through Christ our [my] Lord. Amen.

CHAPTER 7

Caution about Maundy Thursday Passover Seders

JON M. SWEENEY

As we've said, the familiar proper nouns "Old Testament" and "New Testament" are problematic. They lead Christians to assume there was an old covenant God made with the people Israel, followed by a new covenant God made with the church, and the adjectives "old" and "new" lead us to think of the "old" as having been replaced by the "new." The official doctrine of most of our churches used to tell us to think precisely in those terms. We now know better, but only recently has the change become official. (See chapter 5, "Supersessionism/Replacement Theology," by Richard Lux.)

But we still need to get the word out.

When it comes to Christians performing certain Jewish rituals, there are other things to be careful of. The way we call our scriptures "New" and Jewish scriptures "Old" is a problem of finding *too much* difference between the Testaments; but when it comes to Christians having Passover Seders in church or in Christian homes, problems can arise from finding *too little* difference between the faiths.

This problem has plagued and followed Christians since the fourth century when Emperor Constantine made Christianity not only legal but the official religion of the empire. Since then, in most parts of the world, there has been a sense of—at the risk of putting it too crudely—*We won!* So we are in a position to pick and choose those bits and pieces from other religious and cultural traditions that appeal to us, as if they are ours to plunder. It isn't always "plundering"; sometimes we do this out of deep appreciation and a desire to learn and grow in our faith. But we have to be careful. In the last few generations, as Christians have become more familiar and neighborly with people of other religious traditions, we've extended that familiarity to appreciation, and sometimes appreciation becomes appropriation.

For example, this happens when we decide that a Native American ritual would work nicely inside a Christian ritual. This happens when we add an expression or practice from Buddhism into our Christian prayer life. These appropriations are usually harmless to the other religious traditions, but they are not always so. Sometimes it can feel like something precious has been stolen from them.

I remember asking a rabbi friend twenty some years ago why he was troubled by Christians performing Passover Seders in their homes. It is an opportunity for Christians to come to better understand the Jewish roots of their faith. He responded, "It has to be done with sensitivity and a sense of proper boundaries. Otherwise, it's offensive. How would you feel, for instance, if I decided that the Catholic Mass was lovely and that I would start incorporating a bit of consecrated host into my Kabbalat Shabbat services? If you take 'just a bit' of my Jewish practice, and incorporate it as your own, it is like me taking a nibble of the host." He was overstating to make his point, but it worked. Since then I've wanted to be scrupulous when adopting or observing religious practices from traditions that are not my own.

Christians will sometimes host Passover Seders in their homes or churches. In most cases, this doesn't mean that the Christians are observing the eight days of Passover along with their Jewish friends and neighbors. Rather, Christians usually put on a Seder out of a desire to recall, mark, or celebrate the Jewish origins of Christian faith.

Maundy Thursday—the evening before Good Friday—is the most common day and time for Christians to host a Seder. This is because there is widespread belief that the Last Supper—

which took place on the evening before Jesus was crucified —
was a Seder meal. The Gospels say that Jesus was in Jerusalem
for Passover.

Sometimes a local rabbi will be invited to come lead the
Seder, and in such cases, my concerns of misappropriation are
calmed. The rabbi will know what to do. (Unless, perhaps, it is
a "Messianic rabbi.")[1] But when there is not a rabbi or an experienced Jewish leader for the Seder, then the Christians who are
doing this Jewish ceremony need to be careful.

Follow some guidelines in your Passover Seder:

Don't reappropriate the symbols and texts to Christian uses.
For example, some Christians want to say that the matzoh
(unleavened bread) that's central and symbolic in a Jewish Seder
is representative of Jesus's body. The Gospel of John suggests
this, when John 1:29 refers to Jesus as the "Lamb of God." But
this is to radically change the meaning of matzoh as understood
in a Seder. If you are hosting or participating in a Seder, you
should do so by honoring the order and meaning of this ritual
meal that is not yours. Drawing parallels is okay; go ahead and
talk about the Christian parallels and ways of understanding
unleavened bread, including how Christians use unleavened
bread sacramentally, but do not simply reappropriate the Jewish symbol and texts.

The same goes for wine that is part of a traditional Seder.
Four cups of wine are drunk to remember different teachings of
the Seder. Christians might want to say that the wine represents
the blood of Christ on the cross. But it doesn't. At least it doesn't
in the context of a Jewish Seder. Again, discussing parallels is
fine, but this is a matter of balance and tact; don't simply "take
over" the symbolism and change it. Allow yourself to learn a
Seder as it is, and what it means in the context of the original
Passover story, in Judaism.

---

1. It's complicated. "Messianic" and "Jewish" don't go together in modern
Judaism. You'll find, undoubtedly, that your Messianic Jewish friends relate
well with Christians, but not with Jews. This is because to be Messianic Jewish
is to be Christian in the eyes of Jewish people today.

Jesus was a teacher of Torah when he responded to the lawyer in Luke 10. Jesus asked him, "What is written in the law. What do you read there?" The lawyer replies with excellent Torah teaching: "You shall love the Lord your God with all your heart, and with all your soul, and with all your strength, and with all your mind; and your neighbor as yourself." And Jesus says, yes. "Do this, and you will live" (Luke 10:26–28 NRSV).

Chapter 8

For When We Hear "Crucify him!" on Good Friday

Jon M. Sweeney

Each year, I go to church on Good Friday with mixed emotions. I have my Christian desire to be present and a witness to what happened to Christ, and I feel dread at the impact that I know the performance of the Good Friday Gospel reading has on many who hear it. I often express my concerns to friends. I've even been known to implore my clergy to reconsider using St. John's Gospel for the Good Friday reading.

As you may know, especially if you worship in a tradition like mine, the Good Friday reading is not usually just a reading. It is a performance. This is the only time each year that we do this in my church—*perform* the Gospel with multiple lectors, or "actors," taking parts in the Passion Narrative, making it come alive as it is read aloud. (For this reason, when I sometimes say, *Could we not do it this way?*, friends will respond, *But, I love it!*)

The Good Friday reading-performance can be powerful. When it is done well, it is done very well. The effects of that performance then mirror my mixed emotions on being there to witness it: I feel the passion of my faith, but I also feel the heat of what has inflamed antisemitism for centuries. The effect of the Good Friday performance of St. John's Gospel can be like the effect that Passion plays have had on small communities for centuries: inflaming already-rooted antisemitic attitudes with what people hear as God's truth.

We need context. Most of all, we need to listen to our church leaders, who have already reflected over the last half-century on the necessary context. And we need to ask them to give us this proper context at the moment, on the very day, when this Gospel reading is performed. In my tradition, Roman Catholicism, all this wisdom is already "out there" and available. (It is also explained in several of the chapters of this book.) For example:

1. "What happened in (Christ's) passion cannot be blamed on all the Jews then living without distinction nor on the Jews of today," especially since "authorities of the Jews and those who followed their lead pressed for the death of Christ."[1]
2. Christ in his boundless love freely underwent his passion and death because of the sins of all men, so that all might attain salvation.[2]
3. The *Catechism* of the Council of Trent teaches that Christian sinners are more to blame for the death of Christ than those few Jews who brought it about – they indeed "knew not what they did" (cf. Luke 23:24), and we know it only too well.[3]
4. In the same way and for the same reason, "the Jews should not be presented as repudiated or cursed by God, as if such views followed from the holy Scriptures," even though it is true that "the Church is the new people of God" (*Nostra Aetate* 4).[4]

Most of all, I want to remind each one of us in church on Good Friday of what no. 3 clearly says: *We* are the ones who are to blame for the crucifixion and death of Jesus. For those of

---

1. Commission for Religious Relations with the Jews, "Guidelines and Suggestions for Implementing the Conciliar Declaration *Nostra Aetate.*"

2. Commission for Religious Relations with the Jews, "Notes on the Correct Way to Present the Jews and Judaism in Preaching and Catechesis in the Roman Catholic Church."

3. Ibid.

4. Ibid.

us who look to Christ for salvation, this is the very crux of our faith. Someone else is not to blame; we are the ones who made Christ's death on the cross necessary.

So if you like the Gospel performance as it is often done at the Good Friday service, and you like the part where the crowd—described (and performed) as "The Jews"—yells out, "Crucify him! Crucify him!," then I suggest this year, perhaps for the first time, you realize that you were one of the ones in the crowd that day yelling those words. If that happens, then I love it too.

CHAPTER 9

The Great Commandment

ROBERT ELLSBERG

I heard a sermon many years ago that left a great impression. In my memory it consisted of only one sentence, though perhaps that is simply the only line I recall: "There are two kinds of people in the Gospels: the Good Religious People, and the sinners, whom Jesus loved." Perhaps that oversimplifies the matter. But it is a sermon I never forgot, and I think it is relevant to this volume.

The fact that Jesus's preaching and practice provoked opposition is one of the consistent motifs of the Gospels. Some of this undoubtedly came from Jesus's challenge to the status quo. Prophets have a habit of making enemies, especially among the powerful. But a good deal of his opposition evidently came from sincere fellow Jews who took their faith seriously. They accused Jesus of being casual or lax in observing religious laws; of violating purity codes; of consorting with sinners, outsiders, or unclean persons. Jesus himself seems to have deliberately triggered such reactions—conspicuously reaching out to people of suspect reputation, invoking the examples of Samaritans and other "outsiders" as examples of true devotion, constantly emphasizing the practice of mercy as the highest meaning of the law.

While this undoubtedly offended certain Good Religious People, it was hardly a rejection of Jewish faith. Jesus stood squarely in the tradition of the Hebrew prophets who excoriated the notion that mere obedience to the law or correct liturgical practices were a substitute for justice or the practice of mercy. When Jesus describes the "great commandment" as loving God and loving one's neighbor (on these "depend all the law and the prophets"), he is standing squarely in the Pharisaic school of Hillel. Even "the scribe" who had put the question to him responds approvingly: "You are right, Teacher; you have truly said that he is one, and there is no other but he; and to love him with all the heart and with all the understanding and with all the strength, and to love one's neighbor as oneself, is much more than all whole burnt offerings and sacrifices" (Mark 12:32–33).

Nevertheless, if Jesus's differences were not with "the Jews" or Pharisees, as such, there is no doubt that he publicly challenged certain attitudes: legalism, hypocrisy, exclusivism, chauvinism, self-righteousness. These are not singularly "Jewish" or "Pharisaic" attitudes. They were—and are—among the particular temptations or occupational hazards of those who take their religion most seriously. In his parable of the "Good Samaritan," it is not by accident that Jesus highlights a despised "outsider" in the role of hero, while observing that it is a "priest and a Levite" who pass the injured man on the side of the road.

It is, however, to miss the whole meaning of the story when Christians somehow appropriate to themselves the role of the hero, in contrast with the "hypocritical Jews." In telling such stories, Jesus was, of course, addressing an audience entirely comprised of fellow Jews. In a Christian retelling of the story, the terms would have to be transposed: thus, it would be a bishop, a doctor of divinity, or a canon lawyer who pass the man on the side of the road. And as for the "Samaritan"—a name that no longer evokes a shudder of distaste—we would have to select a different candidate from among our own categories of despised outsider.

Yes, it is undoubtedly true that among many of the Good Religious People of his day, Jesus provoked opposition. That is not hard to believe, nor does it entail antisemitic bias, as long as it does not imply a particular judgment against Jews or Judaism. Woven into the very DNA of the religious imagination is the temptation to believe that only we, the *true believers,* the pious ones, the truly devout, are God's favorites—not like those others: the heretics, the unbelievers, the lax, the impure, the *sinners.* Jesus, the Jewish teacher and prophet, challenged such attitudes among his own. Yet in projecting such criticism onto "the Jews," Christians have entirely missed the point of his message. Not only would this become a basis for persecuting Jews, but it has ensured that Christians would shield themselves from the prophetic scrutiny of Jesus's teaching.

Thus, Christians could suppose that, whereas Jews follow a religion "of laws," *we* follow a religion of *love,* that we—unlike *those others*—observe the spirit and not the mere letter of the law. Every Sunday we could safely rejoice in hearing tales of Jesus's rhetorical triumph over the scribes and Pharisees, never imagining that his words might be addressed to us: our own capacity for judgment, self-righteousness, and hard-heartedness. (As for our "religion of love," we dared not boast of that to the victims of pogroms and the Inquisition, the casualties of religious wars, and all those condemned in the name of our own intricate religious laws and purity codes.)

It turns out there are Good Religious People in every religion. The issue is not whether religious people can be "good," or whether concern for doctrines, religious codes, or liturgical rules necessarily implies hypocrisy—but the attitude of those so convinced of their own goodness, possession of the truth, and closeness to God that they can see nothing but the error and sins of everyone around them, and thus are incapable of heeding the "great commandment."

In the early days of his papacy, Pope Francis caused wonder and scandal on Holy Thursday when he washed the feet of the inmates in a prison he visited, including women and Muslims. When he said of homosexuals, "Who am I to judge?," many Catholics were outraged. When he suggested introducing a more clement attitude toward the divorced and remarried, there were those who openly muttered that the pope was teetering on the edge of heresy. In short, Pope Francis has faced opposition from many Good Religious People, including scribes and clergy from his own church, and for reasons not unlike the controversy that Jesus encountered: because of his scandalous mercy, because he seems to emphasize the spirit over the letter of the law, because he suggests that God's love is not the special property of Christians. Nor is this simply a Catholic problem. There are Good Religious People among Protestants of every stripe, as there are among Hindus, Buddhists, Muslims, and Jews.

It has taken the monstrous violence of the last century for Christians to revise their teachings about the Jews. Much remains to be done. The memory that Jesus was himself a Jew is an important starting point. But that is only a beginning. It still remains for Christians to look in the mirror and ask whether they see themselves among the Good Religious People or among the sinners, whom Jesus loved.

CHAPTER 10

Why We Need to Translate
Ioudaioi as "Judeans"

WES HOWARD-BROOK

"This here's Stan the Man Uris," Richie told Ben. "Stan's a Jew. Also, he killed Christ. At least that's what Victor Criss told me one day."

"I think that must have been my father," Stan said.

— Stephen King, *It*

As a kid who grew up in a nearly all-Jewish neighborhood in Los Angeles in the early 1960s, I was terrified of Christians. Not that I knew any directly. But what I had heard was that Christians thought that I, as a Jew, was responsible for the death of Jesus Christ. Given that, at the time, Jews were about 2 percent of the U.S. population, this meant that I was afraid that I could be a victim of nearly anyone I ran into outside of my little pocket of Jewish identity.

And my fear was not completely irrational. Until the Vatican II document *Nostra Aetate*, the official position of the Roman Catholic Church was that all Jews were condemned by God. While official church teachings on Jews and antisemitism may have gone through what some have called a "revolution" at the council, this change has not filtered into English-language translations of the Bible, and thus, not into the hearts and minds of many Catholics and other Christians.

So what do the Gospels say about "Jews" and the death of Jesus? The simple, if perhaps not sufficient, answer, is, nothing at all. The New Testament was written in the language of *koine* ("common") Greek. The words "Jews" and "Judaism" are part of the English language. Thus, two millennia of Christian anti-Judaism,[1] as experienced by English speakers/readers today, is a function of translation, not the original text itself.

The *koine* Greek word frequently rendered in English as "Jew" is *Ioudaios*, and for "Jews," *Ioudaioi*. What did this word mean at the time of Jesus and the New Testament writers? What might the relationship be between Jesus's opponents and today's "Jews"?

One of the challenges in addressing these questions is that for us the word "Jew(s)" is highly ambiguous. Does it identify one's religion? One's ethnicity? One's place of origin or of residence? More than one of the above? How can one decide what identifying someone as a Jew is telling us about who that person is?

The ancient world hardly knew these categories. In many ways, the very idea of a religion as a set of beliefs and practices that anyone can take up or take with them is a modern invention.[2] Similarly, we divide forms of group identity into two categories that, for the ancients, were one: ethnicity and nationhood. That is, one can be, for example, ethnically Mexican but also be a citizen of the United States. But in the New Testament, the Greek *ethnos* is generally translated as "nation" (e.g., Romans 4:17). This can become very confusing for we who unconsciously read according to our own cultural presuppositions.

Thus, our first step in seeking to answer the questions posed above is to enter into the cultural contexts of the biblical authors and characters. Consider, for example, the genealogy of Jesus

---

1. "Anti-Judaism" is the more precise term for hatred of or opposition to "Jews," as opposed to the more common "antisemitism," which is a wider category that includes all peoples of Semitic origin, including Arabs.

2. Carlin A. Barton and Daniel Boyarin, *Imagine No Religion: How Modern Abstractions Hide Ancient Realities* (New York: Fordham University Press, 2016).

in Matthew 1. It begins by describing Jesus as "the son of David, the son of Abraham." Abraham was from Ur in Chaldea, also known as "Babylonia" (Genesis 11:27–31). His obedient response to the call of a god named YHWH did not change his essential identity, according to the Genesis narrative, other than to have his name changed by YHWH from "Abram" to "Abraham" (Genesis 17:5). In other words, Abraham was not a "Jew" before or after his encounter with YHWH. He was simply a person from Babylon who sought to obey the reality he knew as YHWH (among other names for God in Genesis).

It is only with his and Sarah's descendants that the Bible develops a collective name for those who are in relationship with YHWH. Their grandson Jacob has his name changed to "Israel" by a mysterious middle-of-the-night wrestler (Genesis 32:28; see also 35:10, where "God" affirms this name change). It is his children (from four women) who become known collectively as the "Israelites" (Hebrew, *bene yisrael*, literally, "sons of Israel"). In its original sense, the meaning is genealogical: the people who descend by birth from Jacob/Israel. And yet, the biblical authors refer to these people by other names too: "Jacob" or "house of Jacob" (e.g., Exodus 19:3; Isaiah 9:8) and "Ephraim" (literally, a son of Jacob's own son, Joseph, Genesis 41:52; Jeremiah 31:18, 20; Hosea 4:17).

This becomes even more complicated when one considers the history of the double monarchy described in the Bible: one of "Israel" and the other of "Judah" (Hebrew, *yehudah*). The label "Judah" is also ambiguous. It refers first to one of Jacob's sons (Genesis 29:35), but later, to the southern kingdom with its capital in Jerusalem. There is no particular reason to associate the place "Judah" with the descendants of the son of Jacob, Judah. Most scholars today would agree that neither designation, "Israelites" or "Judahites," refers to people who share a genealogical history. Rather, these labels come to refer to people who are bound by covenant to YHWH of whatever "ethnic" origin who lived in the northern or southern regions of Canaan/Palestine, respectively.

The Israelite monarchy collapsed in 722 BCE under the hand of the Assyrians. Like most empires, then and now, the Assyrians were concerned about ethnic/national solidarity as a source of resistance to their rule. To seek to dilute this unity, the Bible reports that they brought in peoples from five different "nations" to intermarry with the Israelites (2 Kings 17:24–41). The outcome was that the designation "Israelites" for the people of that region was eventually replaced by the name of the capital city of the former monarchy: Samaria, and hence, "Samaritans."

While the southern monarchy held out against the Assyrians, a century later the Babylonians invaded and destroyed Jerusalem in 586 BCE, bringing the elite into exile in Babylon. Much of the Hebrew Bible struggles with this catastrophe. As we hear a psalmist cry, "How could we sing the Lord's song in a foreign land?" (Psalm 137:4). It is likely that over the fifty years of exile, many people who had identified as "Judahites" settled into their new home, becoming "Babylonians." Others, however, took advantage of the defeat of the Babylonians by the Persians and sought to return to Judah to rebuild Jerusalem and the temple.

The Persians referred to the portion of the "Province Beyond the River" occupied by the former exiles as "Yehud." Thus, the Hebrew text calls those people "Yehudi" (e.g., Ezekiel 4:12). The New Revised Standard Version renders this in English as "Jews." For the priest-scribe Ezra, who led the mission to restore Jerusalem and the temple, the label is explicitly what we would call "ethnic." He laments with torn garments and outcry what he sees as the greatest of all sins: "the holy seed has mixed itself with the peoples of the land" (Ezra 9:2–4). He goes on to prohibit intermarriage between Yehudi and outsiders as the key commitment of the renewed national identity in the ancient location (9:12–14).

The story continues some two hundred years later with the conquests of Alexander the Great in the fourth century BCE. Alexander was a Greek-speaking Macedonian. Thus, with his conquests, both the Greek language and the cultural complex known as Hellenism spread across the Mediterranean and beyond. One result was the translation of the Hebrew Scriptures into Greek, aka the Septuagint. It was this text, not the original Hebrew texts, that was used by Greek-speaking New Testament writers as they sought to fit the Jesus story into this complex of traditions.

And it is with the Septuagint that we first find the Greek *Ioudaios/Ioudaioi* used to refer to the people of God. For some, the biblical traditions could be assimilated to Hellenism. For others, however, such an accommodation was seen as a vile abandonment of all that their ancestors had fought and often died for. We hear the narrator of 1 Maccabees express it like this:

> In those days there appeared in Israel transgressors of the law who seduced many, saying: "Let us go and make a covenant with the Gentiles all around us; since we separated from them, many evils have come upon us." (1 Maccabees 1:11)

The Maccabean narrator's perspective, however, was hardly that of all the people in the land. The result was a simultaneous war in the early second century BCE against the successors of Alexander known as the "Seleucids" and a civil war among the *Ioudaioi* (e.g., 1 Maccabees 2:23; 8:20–23). Thus, we see that from the outset, the word *Ioudaioi* is a contested one, with various persons and factions claiming over time to be the true *Ioudaioi*. In the absence of a hierarchical infrastructure, there was no way to decide who was officially right.

A century after this war, the Romans in 67 BCE took direct control of Jerusalem and what they now called Judea. Later, they installed their own agent, Herod the Great, as king of Judea. Not surprisingly, this arrogation of control of Jerusalem by a foreign empire aroused ancient hostilities and a renewed hope for a divinely anointed liberator, a *messiah*.

It is into this conflicted and complex situation that Jesus of Nazareth appeared. This is not the place to rehearse Jesus's message and its mixed reception. What is key here is to explore who the *Ioudaioi* were in this context. Scholars such as Shaye Cohen and Steve Mason have reviewed both biblical and other Greek texts that use this word in the time before and after the New Testament writings. Both writers conclude that "Jews" as a label of personal identity and "Judaism" as a system of beliefs and practices to which "Jews" adhere are anachronistic in this context. They prefer "Judeans" or "Judaeans" to "Jews" as a general translation of *Ioudaioi*.

But if it were only a matter of scholarly accuracy, this essay and book would not be necessary. The problem, of course, is both translating the word as "Jews" and seeing the "Jews" as the enemies of Jesus, and thus of God. The central text from which this deathly combination emerges is the Gospel of John. Of the 195 uses of *Ioudaios/Ioudaioi* in the New Testament, seventy-one are in the Gospel of John.

I carried the childhood fears named at the start of this essay into both my discipleship of Jesus and my work as a biblical exegete. Not surprisingly, then, my first book was a commentary on the Gospel of John, *Becoming Children of God: John's Gospel and Radical Discipleship* (1994). In that book, I sought to show how the *Ioudaioi* in John were neither today's "Jews" nor the ancient world's "Jews." First, they are residents of Judea, just as a "Samaritan" (Greek, *Samaritis*) means a resident of Samaria (e.g., John 4:9) or a "Galilean" (Greek, *Galilaios*) means a resident of Galilee (e.g., John 4:45). But in the narrative context of the Gospel of John, the *Ioudaioi* are those who are ideological defenders and economic beneficiaries of the Roman–Judean collaboration.

Consider this from within the dynamics of Jesus's own identity and ministry in John. He and all those who follow him are people who identified with the traditions of Israel and Judah found in the Scriptures. In other words, none are explicitly called "Gentiles," the designation (from the Latin, *gentilis*, or "same family/clan," but in the New Testament as Greek, *ta ethnē*, "the nations") for all who are not members of the covenanted community. When Jesus gets into arguments with the *Ioudaioi*, he puts the question not in terms of what it means to be *Ioudaioi* but rather "children of Abraham" (e.g., 8:33–58). The Jesus in John's Gospel is not in any way "anti-Jewish." What he opposes is claiming that one is being faithful to the covenants with Abraham and Moses (e.g., 5:45–47) while practicing murderous violence and deception (e.g., 8:44). In other words, Jesus was not rejecting "Jews" and seeking to replace them with "Christians." He is seeking, like the prophets before him, to call the elite and their supporters to radical reform. We hear a nearly identical call near the start of the Gospel of Luke, in the mouth of John the Baptist:

> John said to the crowds that came out to be baptized by him, "You brood of vipers! Who warned you to flee from the wrath to come? Bear fruits worthy of repentance. Do not begin to say to yourselves, 'We have Abraham as our ancestor'; for I tell you, God is able from these stones to raise up children to Abraham. Even now the ax is lying at the root of the trees; every tree therefore that does not bear good fruit is cut down and thrown into the fire." (Luke 3:7–9)

Neither Jesus in John nor John the Baptist in Luke could imagine God wanting people to abandon the covenant. The opposite is true: they were calling people *back* to the covenant. In other words, the struggle was not in any way between "Jews" and "Christians." It was between different understandings of what it means to be the people of God.

Consider a certain historical parallel from Christian history. When an Augustinian monk named Martin Luther refused to be quiet about the corruptions and doctrinal distortions of the Roman Catholic leadership, was he abandoning Christianity and seeking to start a new religion? Of course not! He was, like Jesus, challenging those leaders to return to the ancient understanding of God's relationship with humanity. While many conservative Protestants may see Roman Catholics as other than Christian, that doesn't make it so. Rather, Luther established a new branch on the ancient tree. The apostle Paul used this same metaphor to describe how the Gentiles could become part of the covenanted people of God: not by leaving the "Jews" behind, but by seeing themselves as grafted onto the one tree (Romans 11).

With Vatican II, the Roman Catholic Church officially gave up its historical hostility to Jews. It is long past time for everyday Catholics and others who claim Jesus as Lord to move past reading Jesus's opponents as "the Jews." In the season of Lent, may we all embrace our membership in the united family of the people of the one God.

Further Reading

Barton, Carlin A., and Daniel Boyarin, *Imagine No Religion: How Modern Abstractions Hide Ancient Realities* (New York: Fordham University Press, 2016).

Cohen, Shaye J. D., *The Beginnings of Jewishness: Boundaries, Varieties, Uncertainties* (Berkeley: University of California Press, 2001).

Howard-Brook, Wes, *Becoming Children of God: John's Gospel and Radical Discipleship* (Eugene, OR: Wipf & Stock, 2003).

Mason, Steve, "Jews, Judaeans, Judaizing, Judaism: Problems of Categorization in Ancient History," *Journal for the Study of Judaism* 38, no. 4 (2007): 457–512.

———, "Ancient Jews or Judeans? Different Questions, Different Answers," *Marginalia* | *Los Angeles Review of Books*, https://marginalia.lareviewofbooks.org/ancient-jews-judeans-different-questions-different-answers-steve-mason.

CHAPTER 11

From the "Teaching of Contempt" to Nostra Aetate: The Shift of Vatican II on the Relations with the Jews

MASSIMO FAGGIOLI

Anti-Jewish Christian theology (Catholic, but also Protestant and Eastern Orthodox) perpetuated for centuries, and was one of the roots of, the antisemitic persecutions of Jews that took place in Europe leading to the Holocaust during World War II. In the early post–World War II period the issue of the responsibility of Christians for the persecution of Jews was particularly sensitive for Catholics in light of the institutional dimension and centralized structures of the Roman Catholic Church: the initial endorsement of Fascism and even Nazism by many Catholic leaders; the role of the papacy and the diplomatic service of the Vatican during the dictatorship in Italy and Germany, and during the Second World War; and the emerging, delicate issue of the relationship with the newly created (1948) State of Israel where a significant minority of Catholics lived in an often-precarious political situation, protected by regimes that were in conflict with the Jewish state.

These reasons were among the most important for why the agenda of the Second Vatican Council, announced by John XXIII in January 1959, initially did not have in mind a document on the Jews. After the war, there had been discussions in intellectual circles (especially in North America, France, Germany, the Netherlands, and Switzerland) about the significance of the Holocaust for theology, but they had not affected the institutional and theological headquarters of Catholicism, Rome and the Vatican. One clear sign of change took place on March 21, 1959, when John XXIII decided to change the prayer for the Jews during the liturgy of Good Friday, abolishing the disparaging Latin words *perfidis* ("faithless") and *iudaicam perfidiam* ("perfidious Jews").

That was the first episode of change in Catholic teaching regarding Jews at Vatican II, and John XXIII played a key role. In fact, a document on the Jews "would not have been considered at all without the direct intervention of John XXIII."[1] Another decisive moment took place on June 13, 1960, when John XXIII had an audience with the French historian Jules Isaac, who had lost his entire family to the extermination camps in Germany (except son Jean-Claude, who survived Auschwitz and a death march in January 1945) and had published the book *Jésus et Israël* (1948). Isaac explained the impact on the Christian psyche of what he called "the teaching of contempt" against the Jews. He recommended to John XXIII the institution of a commission to study the question: "The pope reacted immediately, saying, 'This is what I have been thinking from the beginning of this meeting.' . . . Expressing my gratitude for the welcome received, I wondered if there was a glimmer of hope I could take away. He exclaimed, 'You are entitled to more than a hope!'"[2]

John XXIII had a particular sensitivity to the Jewish people thanks to his experience as a papal diplomat in Bulgaria (1925–1934), Turkey and Greece (1935–1944), and France (1945–1953). While in Turkey he met several times with the Grand Rabbi of Istanbul, Markus, and representatives of the Jewish Agency for Palestine. He also had worked to save the lives of refugees from

---

1. John Connelly, *From Enemy to Brother: The Revolution in Catholic Teaching on the Jews, 1933–1965* (Cambridge, MA: Harvard University Press, 2012), 240.

2. From the diary of Jules Isaac, in Norman C. Tobias, *Jewish Conscience of the Church: Jules Isaac and the Second Vatican Council*, Preface by Gregory Baum (New York: Palgrave Macmillan, 2017), 187–88.

Eastern Europe: Jews, Polish, and Greek refugees.[3] Then in September 1960 John XXIII asked the newly created Secretariat for Christian Unity, led by German Jesuit Cardinal Augustin Bea, to prepare the draft of a document on the Jews. Secretary of State Cardinal Amleto Giovanni Cicognani and the central preparatory commission had excluded the issue from the conciliar agenda for political reasons arising from fears of the reaction of the churches in the Arab countries and of a surge of fundamentalist antisemitism. The explanation given was that if the church had to draft a document on the Jews, it should draft a document on Muslims too.[4] But at the request of John XXIII, the secretariat nevertheless reintroduced it, as a chapter in the draft of the schema on ecumenism.[5]

* * *

At Vatican II, theological, ecclesiastical, and political considerations intersected in the conciliar discussion on the Jews. One important moment was when the statement on the Jews was taken off the council's agenda to allay disquiet after news in June 1962 that the World Jewish Congress had appointed (with the endorsement of Israel's Foreign Ministry and Ministry of Religious Affairs) its own "unofficial observer" at the council. This caused many reactions and political overtones, and the Secretary of State, Cardinal Cicognani, removed the document from the agenda. In December that year, John XXIII accepted Cardinal Bea's request to reintroduce it.

After the election of Pope Paul VI, in June 1963, Cardinal Bea adopted a pragmatic approach in order to have the text of *De Iudaeis* ("The Jews") examined by the council: it could become

---

3. About this see Massimo Faggioli, *John XXIII: The Medicine of Mercy* (Collegeville, MN: Liturgical Press, 2014), 75–78.

4. See Alberto Melloni, "Nostra Aetate, 1965–2005," in *Nostra Aetate: Origins, Promulgation, Impact on Jewish–Catholic Relations*, ed. Neville Lamdan and Alberto Melloni (Berlin: LIT, 2007), 16–20.

5. See *Vatican II: The Complete History of Vatican II*, ed. Alberto Melloni (Mahwah, NJ: Paulist Press, 2015), 224–25; *History of Vatican II*, ed. Giuseppe Alberigo and Joseph Komonchak, 5 vols. (Maryknoll, NY: Orbis Books, 1995–2006).

a chapter of the document on the church or of the document on ecumenism or an appendix to the document on ecumenism. Ultimately, the chapter on the Jews was mostly welcomed by European and North American bishops but met with strong opposition from bishops of the Catholic churches in the Middle East and from the extremist fringes of the conciliar conservative minority.

Fears that the document could be interpreted as a political statement in favor of the State of Israel made clear, by the fall of 1963, that the council could not treat the Jews without treating other non-Christian religions. In addition, Paul VI's pilgrimage to the Holy Land in January 1964 highlighted the delicate nature of the Catholic Church and the Holy See's diplomatic relations with the State of Israel (they would be established only in 1993) and the possible repercussions in the Middle East of a conciliar document on the Jews.

Between the spring and the summer of 1964 the text on the Jews was first scheduled to become part of a separate declaration on non-Christians and then reattached to the schema on ecumenism. Among the most important changes in the text drafted by the secretariat in the spring of 1964 was the decision to eliminate from the text any condemnation of the history of Catholic claims against Jews for "deicide"—a term that does not appear in the final text of *Nostra Aetate*. In the third conciliar period, in September 1964, Cardinal Bea presented a totally new text that was clearly trying to steer conciliar discussion away from the issue of Zionism and the State of Israel but also focusing very much on the issue of the Jews, with marginal attention to other religions.

A reformist majority and conservative minority (especially the traditionalist international group "Coetus Internationalis Patrum"), clashed over the text. And some Arab bishops (such as Mar Ignatius Gabriel I Tappouni, patriarch of Antioch) asked for its removal, due to the political difficulties it would create in the churches of the Middle East. One important leader of the minority (Cardinal Ernesto Ruffini of Palermo) spoke against any document in favor of the Jews for theological reasons that echoed anti-Jewish tropes and the old accusations of "deicide."

Another leader of the conciliar minority, Luigi Maria Carli (bishop of Segni, Italy), published a booklet criticizing the turn of Catholic theology away from "traditional" teaching on the Jews. This is when anti-Jewish leaflets and pamphlets were distributed to council fathers and *periti* in St. Peter's Square.

Immediately after the September 1964 conciliar debate, in October, there was an attempt by the governing bodies of the council, led by the secretary general, Archbishop Pericle Felici, to reduce the text on the Jews from a separate document to a chapter of the constitution on the church. Cardinal Bea's reaction in defense of a separate document dealing with the Jews was successful.[6] At the end of 1964 there were important and secret exchanges of letters between Cardinal Bea, Secretary of State Cardinal Cicognani, and Secretary General of the Council Felici, about the delicate nature of the text.[7]

The third intersession (between the third session of Fall 1964 and the fourth session of Fall 1965) saw other attempts by representatives of Arab countries to interfere with discussion of the text, but also of council fathers of the conservative minority to repeat the accusation of deicide. One consequence of this tense situation was the decision to remove from the text the denial of the guilt of deicide accusations.

But the document remained on the agenda; various efforts with emissaries from the Vatican to the leaders of the churches in the Middle East were successful in assuaging their fears about its possible political consequences. Important input came from exchanges between Cardinal Bea and the American rabbi of Polish origin Abraham J. Heschel; also from bishops representing churches with a significant Jewish population (such as in the United States); but also from Jewish observers who were following closely the conciliar debates and in contact with some leading figures of Vatican II.

---

6. See John W. O'Malley, *What Happened at Vatican II* (Cambridge, MA: Harvard University Press, 2008), 219–26.

7. See Annarita Caponera, "Papers of the Secretariat on Christian Unity on *Nostra Aetate*," in *Nostra Aetate: Origins, Promulgation, Impact on Jewish–Catholic Relations*, ed. Neville Lamdan and Alberto Melloni (Berlin: LIT, 2007), 59–62.

Finally, on October 28, 1965, the proposition that the Jews were not to be regarded as repudiated or cursed by God was accepted by a great majority: with 1,821 affirmative votes, 245 negative, and 14 invalid votes. The final solemn vote on *Nostra Aetate* had 2,221 affirmative votes and 88 no votes. The document achieved a large consensus, but the no votes were among the highest for all the sixteen documents approved by Vatican II.

* * *

There is no understanding of *Nostra Aetate* without seeing the importance of the document for the Jews. The paragraph on the Jews is not just the longest but also is generative for the whole declaration dealing also with Hinduism, Buddhism, and "Muslims" (not Islam).[8]

By the fourth draft, *Nostra Aetate* showed the beginning of a new path, but not the last word of the Catholic Church on the Jews. It was, like all the other texts of Vatican II, the fruit of a compromise after years of debates. Among the changes in the text in the last phase of amendments, one of the most important was the deletion of the verb *damnat* (the council *condemns* antisemitism), which was replaced by the more tenuous *deplorat* ("deplores all hatreds, persecutions, displays of antisemitism"). Some commentators noted that some expressions of *Nostra Aetate* 4 revealed a supersessionist theology. In *Nostra Aetate* there was no request for forgiveness from those who had been persecuted by Christians. Moreover, *Nostra Aetate* could not deal with the issue of the theological meaning of the State of Israel and of the Land for contemporary Judaism.

But the declaration made an enormous step forward toward a new understanding of Jews by the Catholic Church and in

---

8. For an extensive and authoritative commentary, see John M. Oesterreicher (one of the theological consultants at Vatican II and one of the key players in the whole debate), "Declaration on the Relationship of the Church to Non-Christian Religions. Introduction and Commentary," in *Commentary on the Documents of Vatican II*, ed. Herbert Vorgrimler, vol. 3 (New York: Herder & Herder, 1969), 1–136.

making clear the incompatibility of anti-Judaism and antisemitism with Catholic doctrine. *Nostra Aetate* was an indirect but unmistakable acknowledgment of the Shoah and of the responsibilities of anti-Jewish theology and of the Catholic Church in the history of antisemitism. It also puts an end to hoping for conversion of the Jews to the church.

Nevertheless, *Nostra Aetate* had its limits. It dealt with antisemitism but not directly with the more important theological issue of anti-Judaism. And for reasons mentioned above, the conciliar fathers could not agree to address the issue of centuries of "deicide" claims against Jewish people.

For these other issues that *Nostra Aetate* could not address, postconciliar developments in papal teaching were of utmost importance. It also took time to implement the conciliar declaration itself. Only on October 22, 1974, was a new "Commission for the Catholic Church's Religious Relations with the Jews" instituted by Paul VI. In the same year, the Commission published *Guidelines and Suggestions for Implementing the Conciliar Declaration "Nostra Aetate."*

A few years later, with the papacy of John Paul II, an undeniable acceleration in the reception of *Nostra Aetate* took place. A second landmark document was *Notes on the Correct Way to Present the Jews and Judaism in Preaching and Catechesis in the Roman Catholic Church* (1985). Then, during the preparations for the Great Jubilee of 2000, the Commission for the Catholic Church's Religious Relations with the Jews published *We Remember: A Reflection on the Shoah* (1998).

During the pontificate of Pope Francis, the commission published another landmark document in the postconciliar reception of *Nostra Aetate*: *The Gifts and the Calling of God Are Irrevocable" (Rom 11:29): A Reflection on Theological Questions Pertaining to Catholic–Jewish Relations on the Occasion of the 50th Anniversary of "Nostra Aetate"* (2015). *Nostra Aetate* was also the first document of Vatican II that Francis quoted, on March 21, 2013, in an official speech at the beginning of his pontificate.

It has been suggested that while, for Jews, *Nostra Aetate* came too late, "for Catholic theology it came too soon and to this day has not been fully digested."[9] On the other hand, the postconciliar official teaching of the church on the Jews shows clearly how much theological and magisterial development there has been since *Nostra Aetate*.

Nostra Aetate and the Debate on Vatican II Today

The conciliar declaration "On the Relation of the Church to Non-Christian Religions," also known as *Nostra Aetate*, is the shortest of the sixteen final documents of Vatican II. But its length is inversely proportional to its enormous importance in the development of the teaching of the church. In the recent history of the interpretation of Vatican II, we have witnessed the emergence in intra-Catholic debate of a sharp contrast between "hermeneutics of continuity and reform" and "discontinuity and rupture." A neotraditionalist Catholic culture has come to see "continuity," in the sense of continuity of teaching, as the only fundamental marker of catholicity in the interpretation of the theological tradition. This has happened at the expense of the concept of *reform*. But from the point of view of history, it has always been clear that some theological reforms require a certain discontinuity in the teaching of the church. *Nostra Aetate* is one of the conciliar documents that represent a change in the sense of continuity and reform, carrying some degree of discontinuity, particularly in the teaching on the Jews.

Nostra Aetate is also perhaps the most powerful argument against the delegitimization of the event of Vatican II, often pursued by neotraditionalists. The same neotraditionalists have also, particularly in recent years, sought to delegitimize the documents of Vatican II. The rejection of the idea of some necessary discontinuity in the recent tradition and magisterium would silently and incrementally question the understanding of ecumenism and interreligious dialogue that has developed in the church over the last fifty years.

In this ecclesial and theological context, the case of *Nostra*

---

9. Connelly, *From Enemy to Brother*, 245.

Aetate is particularly delicate. On the one hand, the theological rethinking evident in Vatican II can be described as *ressourcement*, going back to the sources of the tradition interpreted comprehensively. In this sense, the "Ur-ressourcement," the original and first going back to the sources, is the new acknowledgment by Catholic theology of the Word of Jesus in the gospel as the first source, and the Jewishness of Jesus. Revoking or simply forgetting this huge step forward in the understanding of the gospel by the Christian tradition would have catastrophic consequences on the theological, intellectual, and spiritual balance of Catholicism and Christianity in general. On the other hand, we cannot separate the ongoing ecclesial lapse in the memory of the importance of Vatican II and of *Nostra Aetate* from the current crisis of the relationship between Catholic theology and modern pluralistic democracies. In other words, Vatican II and its teaching on the Jews are two fundamental, even if hidden, pillars of the acceptance by the Catholic Church of modern religious pluralism within the context of a cultural, social, and political pluralism. That special relationship of otherness between Judaism and Christianity, as a God-given legacy, was rediscovered by Vatican II and remains one of the most important mandates for our generation for the relations between Judaism and Christianity.

CHAPTER 12

Differences among Early Jesus Followers: Paul's Warning to the Thessalonians

BISHOP RICHARD J. SKLBA

Ever since the discovery of the Dead Sea Scrolls in 1947, our understanding of the rich diversity of Jewish religious life in ancient Jerusalem and Judea has been greatly enhanced. The variety of interacting and sometimes rival movements during the first century of our Common Era, each with its own devout following, has become a fascinating field of study. It has revealed the context for the vibrant multifaceted Judaism of its day and the initial appearance of what came to be called Christianity.

The Sadducees, for example, with adherents mostly from prominent priestly families, were committed to the literally interpreted texts of the Torah. They lived beside others, however, who were dedicated to the Pharisaic movement and its concern for the value of oral tradition with a conviction regarding the possibility of human resurrection. Zealots were willing to employ force if needed to reject domination by Rome's army. A surprisingly wide spectrum within Hellenistic Judaism also claimed loyal adherents within the population of Jerusalem. The Essenes felt obliged to leave the Temple, which they saw as utterly defiled, and to establish a quasi-monastic residence down in the salted areas around the Dead Sea as they awaited the appearance of the Righteous Teacher who would establish what would be true Judaism.

Each group gathered around its own synagogue where available and sometimes accepted the presence of God-fearing Gentiles who respected the convictions of its members without adopting the external dietary or physical marks of Judaism. It was a very rich diversity.

That emerging presence of Jewish followers of Jesus hailing him as crucified and risen from the dead added even more controversial diversity to religious life in first-century Judaism. Though Jesus himself had claimed a place within the Pharisaic tradition and entered vigorously all the religious arguments of his day, his followers gradually distanced themselves from their Jewish neighbors. The deepening convictions of early Jewish Christians about the divinity of Jesus led Pharisees to be alarmed, and, conversely, the movement of Jewish groups toward revolution against harsh Roman authorities moved early Christian Jewish communities to see the need to distance themselves, in turn, from the increasingly dangerous politics of first-century Jewish life. Early differences gradually hardened as others took up Saul's prior mantle of using force to establish some degree of Jewish unity and orthodoxy (Acts 9:1–2), fluid as that may have been at the time.

The dramatic movement of young Saul of Tarsus from ardent Pharisaism to a more messianic type of Judaism marked off yet another branch of Jewish life centered on the life and teaching of Jesus from Nazareth. Saul was later called Paulus (Latin and Greek replacing the Hebrew, literally meaning "Shortie"), or Paul, after his dramatic transition from a persecuting Jewish vigilante to a preaching Christian missionary. He wrote from his vantage point in the second stage of the Christian message's development, namely, the postresurrection statements of faith. Paul's letters to the communities he founded around the Mediterranean are filled with his convictions regarding the resurrection of Jesus and its implications both for the life of every individual and for the world in which they lived.

Acts of the Apostles

The Acts of the Apostles describes Paul's journeys as an insight into the early missionary activity of Christians. Written sometime between 80 and 90 CE (nearly a generation after Paul's death in Rome), the work purports to describe Paul's ministry to the Gentiles, based on the initial example of Peter himself (Acts 11–12). The text, claiming careful study of sources (Acts 1:1–4), attempted to document Paul's missionary travels through the Roman Empire from the place of his dramatic conversion on the way to Damascus (9:3–10) and his initial training in Syrian Antioch until his eventual final imprisonment in Rome (28:16–30). The years between those events were filled with countless missionary travels, each somehow at the mandate of the authorities in Damascus (13:1–2).

Paul's first missionary visit to Thessalonica is briefly described as quickly controversial (17:1–9) and is contrasted with a more positive fruitful visit to the neighboring town of Beroea (17:10–14), even though that latter stay also ended in some degree of dissension and departure. Paul is presented in those verses as proceeding immediately to the synagogue in Thessalonica, preaching the Lord's death and resurrection with success among some Jews and Gentile God-fearers including prominent women of the city. After brief activity in the synagogue, Paul is described as having turned to the Gentiles. That sequence reflected the repeated history of Paul's work as presented by Acts. He probably spent several months working with that group in Thessalonica prior to his departure. Acts describes Paul's team as incurring jealous negative reactions from Jewish leaders who accused Paul of subversive political activity (17:5) and maneuvered a fine on the supportive synagogue leaders such as Jason for fomenting civic unrest. Paul and Silas quickly slipped out of town at night and moved down the highway to Beroea (17:10–14). The pattern of Paul's work in Thessalonica was thus stereotypically described and quickly contrasted with a more positive and successful mission in Beroea.

The judgment among scholars today seems to grant basic historicity to the events described in Acts. They acknowledge the account as told in such a way, however, as to remove negative bias toward Roman authorities and ultimately prepare for Paul's eventual arrival in Rome at the end of his life's missionary work. The account insists on presenting an often-repeated model of mission first to the Jews and then to the Gentiles. Difficult to discern at times is a more accurate picture of Paul merely using the synagogue to find those Gentiles who might be open to Paul's invitation to be embraced by God's sovereign action in the world's history. Paul in fact saw his mission as focused on the Gentiles.

Paul's life work, like that of Jesus who had found a base in the more populated mercantile and military crossroads at Capernaum (Mark 1:21), selected urban centers as points of entry into social circles and initial religious springboards for his ministry. He sought households open to be used as places of prayer and catechetical conversation. The account of Paul's missionary journeys in Acts needs to be compared carefully to the picture emerging from his actual letters to the communities he had founded and continued to shepherd from a distance.

Paul's First letter to the Thessalonians

The city of Philippi, from which Paul traveled to Thessalonica some seventy-five miles to the west, was located along the great Roman Egnatian highway, which connected Italy to Byzantium. Philippi claimed only five to ten thousand inhabitants as contrasted with the twenty to thirty thousand estimated as living in Thessalonica at the time. The latter city had been initially founded in 316 BCE by a general of Alexander the Great. Its region called Macedonia eventually became a Roman province in 146 BCE with Thessalonica as its capital. Over the course of time the Thessalonians had received many political and economic privileges from Roman authorities, including freedom from certain taxes and significant political independence. The resident citizens eventually even proclaimed Julius Caesar himself as a god in 27 BCE. It was a grand city and an obvious destination for Paul's early missionary efforts in Greece.

In light of that favorable status, the cult of the goddess Roma was also readily embraced among the pagan religious currents of Thessalonica. Unfortunately, an extensive tragic fire in 1917 destroyed most of the city, and the city's speedy rebuilding as a viable port has made new archaeological excavation difficult if not impossible for today's experts. We do know, however, that the residents of first-century Thessalonica heartily embraced the ancient cults of Egyptian deities such as Serapis and Isis together with the Greek figures of Dionysius and the mystery cult of Cabirus, to which Roma and Caesar were added. All that represented the extended pagan religious milieu into which Paul came.

The arrival of Paul's missionary team to Thessalonica probably occurred in late 49 or early 50 CE. After several months of active catechesis there, because of some initial controversy Paul felt obliged to leave town for Corinth from which he then wrote to his former friends and converts. With pastoral concern for the welfare of the little group of converts he had abruptly left behind, Paul quickly sent a delegate from Corinth to demonstrate his enduring affection for the Thessalonians, and to bring back news of their situation.

Upon receiving Timothy's report, Paul wrote his first letter to the Thessalonians. That message expressed prayers of affection and gratitude for them and cautioned them not to be swayed by the words of their former pagan neighbors or any more rigorous followers of Jesus who were undercutting Paul's catechesis by insisting that converts accept the full range of Jewish practices in order to become true disciples of Jesus.

Paul began his letter with an effusive prayer of thanks for the faith, love, and hope that filled the lives of his new converts (1:2–9). The community members to whom Paul addressed his letter were primarily Gentiles, as evidenced by Paul's acknowledgment of their having "turned from idols" to faith in Jesus (v. 9). He noted their eager expectation of the imminent return of the risen Jesus (v. 10) and continued to express gratitude for

the way he had been able to experience their devotion personally. In that social context of new fervor, Paul had labored to
sustain himself without financial burden to the new community
of followers of Jesus who had become truly worthy of God's
invitation into his enduring kingdom (v. 12).

The specific issue to which we address ourselves in this
essay concerns Paul's description of the persecution and hardship being experienced by the young converts whom he had left
behind at Thessalonica. The verses in question come from the
heart of his letter:

> For you, brothers, have become imitators of the Churches
> of God that are in Judea in Christ Jesus. For you suffer the
> same things from your compatriots as they did from the
> Jews, who killed both the Lord Jesus and the prophets and
> persecuted us; they do not please God and are opposed
> to everyone, trying to prevent us from speaking to the
> Gentiles that they may be saved, thus constantly filling up
> the measure of their sins. But the wrath of God has finally
> begun to come upon them. (1 Thessalonians 2:14–16)

Just as Jewish Christians in Jerusalem had experienced resistance from other Jewish leaders, Paul is complaining here about
new arrivals from Jerusalem with whom he has serious disagreements. He lists five accusations against their conduct in
Judea: (1) they killed Christ Jesus, (2) killed prophets, (3) persecuted the followers of Jesus severely, (4) did not truly please
God, and (5) tried to prevent contact with Gentiles.

It would seem, however, that the established Jewish community in Thessalonica itself had not bothered very much with this
new Jewish sect of messianic followers of Jesus. The main local
opponents were former pagan neighbors, labeled as "compa-
triots" (v. 14) who objected to the absence of the new followers of Jesus from the religious rites of social life in a flourishing
city like Thessalonica. Suddenly they felt personally snubbed
but also somehow endangered by these followers of Jesus
who chose not to offer proper civic respect toward the divine
emperor on whose beneficence they depended. Gentiles were

persecuted by fellow Gentiles who became agents of the "distress" (the word in Paul's Greek is *thlipsis*) that they now experienced (2:14; 3:3, 7). Thus it would seem that the basic local opposition to the disciples of Paul at Thessalonica was more political than religious, but real nonetheless.

The fundamental question, here, is the degree to which an anti-Jewish attitude permeated Paul's approach to his mission and his relationship to the young community at Thessalonica. The common conviction of scholars seems to be that the persecution experienced by the early Christians at Thessalonica was from their own former pagan Gentile neighbors. This was similar, Paul pointed out, to the persecution of Jewish Christians from their Jewish neighbors back in Palestine. Gentile Christians were being opposed and even persecuted by others who resented their absence from the civic religious rites that characterized life in Roman cities. Paul, Jewish Christian that he was, laments the opposition his colleagues had experienced from other Jews during his earlier life. The main focus of Paul's teaching at Thessalonica, however, was the imminent return of the Risen Lord (4:14).

It was a fundamental rule of early Christian life that they found in each other's company the basic social community that constituted human existence. They gathered for communal meals and joyfully prayed into the dawn. Their social cohesion, however, aroused suspicions of nefarious secret conduct and rituals hostile to civilized urban living. Jewish visitors from other communities who complained about these secret Christian gatherings only intensified the suspicion of their Gentile neighbors in Thessalonica. The opposition, however, seems to have come primarily from Gentile neighbors, not Jewish, and was marginally supported by Jewish travelers from Jerusalem.

Although some recent scholars[1] have claimed that 1 Thessalonians 4:14–16 is a later anti-Jewish insertion into the text of Paul's letter, most contemporary commentators see it as inte-

---

1. Birger Pearson, "1 Thessalonians 2:13–16: A Deutero-Pauline Interpolation," *Harvard Theological Review* 64 (1971): 79–94.

gral to Paul's original communication. Part of Paul's catechesis, based on the death and resurrection of Jesus, stressed that
the inevitable *thlipsis* (pressure, affliction, and hardship) was
associated with the Christian life of hardship experienced by
all who passed into resurrection and the initial fullness of life
through baptism.

In verse 16, as cited above, Paul makes reference to the wrath
of God that had finally come upon some of the Jewish people
living in Judea. He attacks and dismisses that group of fellow
Jews who were of a different persuasion, and refers to what
they had suffered earlier. There is no need to presume that this
is a reference to the final destruction of Jerusalem by Roman
armies in 70 CE, as some modern commentators would have it.
The Jewish community in Judea had already experienced severe
bloody persecution from Roman authorities. As Josephus had
reported, an initial rebellion among Jewish leaders after 48 CE
had resulted in the massacre of twenty to thirty thousand Jewish inhabitants.[2] That experience of God's wrath was only a
portion of the final judgment that Paul and his generation of
believers in Jesus anticipated for the whole world. Paul's eschatological assumptions saw all those events as part of God's final
assessment of the world.

In a final flourish of magisterial assurance, Paul concludes
his letter with some words of comfort regarding the imminent
return of Jesus. He offers general exhortations toward the moral
life he had described for them when he was still in their midst
(4:1–12 and 5:12–22). Having received Timothy's report on the
state of things in Thessalonica, Paul encourages them to remain
busy as they awaited the final climax of human history. They
were apparently unsettled, however, because a few had died
prior to the return of Jesus in glory, and they feared that their
beloved friends might therefore be excluded from the cosmic
victory they all anticipated. Paul opines that perhaps the dead
will rise first (4:16), and then all the remaining believers will
be swept up into final glory forever. His words represented a

---

2. Josephus, *Antiquities of the Jews* 20.112, and *Bellum Judaicum* 2.224–27.

pastoral effort to restore religious serenity to his recent converts back home. Paul, eschatological Jewish believer that he was, remained convinced that any and all tribulations experienced in Thessalonica would ultimately be utterly insignificant at the final consummation of the world and the triumph of God's kingdom.

Paul went on to a life of evangelizing other Gentile and Jewish communities in the larger cities of the Roman Empire as witnessed by the collection of letters eventually accredited to his name. As the years passed, Paul seemed no longer driven by the immediacy of the Lord's return. He found a new reference point for his later preaching and teaching in the life and witness of Abraham, whose faith became a blessing for both Hebrew descendants and their Gentile neighbors (Genesis 12:1–3; 15:6; Galatians 3:6). Eventually his letter to the Romans gave testimony to the abiding place of Israel in God's plans for the salvation of the world, for "the gifts and call of God are irrevocable" (Romans 11:29).

Almost two thousand years later, Paul's conviction continues to give hope to Jews and Gentiles alike who still await God's final victory of faith, love, and hope.[3]

---

3. In writing this essay, I carefully consulted these volumes: Raymond Collins, *Studies on the First Letter to the Thessalonians*, Bibliotheca Ephemeridum Theologicarum Lovaniensium 66 (Leuven: University Press, 1984); Robert Jewett, *The Thessalonian Correspondence: Pauline Rhetoric and Millenarian Piety* (Philadelphia: Fortress Press, 1986); Todd Still, *Conflict at Thessalonica: A Pauline Church and Its Neighbors*, Journal for the Study of the New Testament Supplement Series 183 (Sheffield: Sheffield Academic Press, 1999); Karl Paul Donfried, *Paul, Thessalonians and Early Christianity* (Grand Rapids, MI: Eerdmans, 2002); Gary Shogren, *I & II Thessalonians*, Exegetical Commentary on the New Testament (Grand Rapids, MI: Zondervan, 2012); and Gerd Lüdemann, *The Earliest Christian Text: 1 Thessalonians* (Salem, OR: Polebridge Press, 2013).

CHAPTER 13

"For Fear of the Jews": Antisemitism in John's Time and in Ours

GREG GARRETT

It's the second Sunday of Easter, which my friend Rowan Williams rightly calls "Rector's Holiday," and so I find myself climbing into the pulpit again as the church staff take some well-deserved rest.

I've been in the congregation throughout Holy Week, listened to the performance of the Good Friday Passion Narrative from the Gospel of John, which features "the Jews" calling for the death of Jesus. This morning, as every Easter 2, the Gospel lesson from which I preach is also from the Gospel of John, a familiar reading that has to do with the disciple we sometimes call Doubting Thomas and the aftermath of Jesus's death and resurrection; and early in the reading, we hear this verse: "When it was evening on that day, the first day of the week, and the doors of the house where the disciples had met were locked for fear of the Jews, Jesus came and stood among them and said, 'Peace be with you'" (John 20:19 NRSV).

Right there, parenthetically wedged into this story about resurrection, we discover that the disciples are hiding behind closed doors because they are afraid of "the Jews."

It's a moment, like others in the Gospel of John, that is not always remarked on from the pulpit. Looking over a dozen years of preaching on Easter 2, I see that there were years when I skipped straight over the fear of the Jews on the way to doubt or faith or epiphany or commitment or any of the other big spiritual lessons that that particular community seemed to need on that particular second Sunday of Easter.

But in the past few years, anytime we encounter one of these parenthetical statements about "the Jews" in a Gospel reading (particularly in John) I have taken to highlighting them, at the very least, as major sources of Christian antisemitism, and sometimes I have devoted substantial space to correcting bad readings and refuting this prejudice, the twin impulses that are at the heart of this essay.

* * *

First and foremost, "fear of the Jews" is a ridiculous and inaccurate statement of why the followers of Jesus are gathered behind locked doors in the Gospel lesson. These men are themselves Jews. All of them. Peter is a Jew. Thomas is a Jew. The risen Jesus, the Anointed One who steps miraculously into their midst, is a Jew. In fact, as has been mentioned elsewhere in this book, virtually every character in the Gospel of John with a speaking part, almost everyone in Jesus's story, is a Jew.

The disciples are not afraid of the Jews per se. That would just be silly, like groundhogs being frightened by their own shadows. The disciples are Jews, their families are Jews, their friends are Jews. The world of John, this narrative in which they work and play and pray, is Jewish. It is an unhistorical reading of the Gospel of John to imagine that Jesus and his disciples are, like later readers, "Christians" at odds with "the Jews." In this story where Peter and Thomas and Jesus are characters somewhere in the early 30s CE, the word "Christian" hasn't been introduced yet, and non-Jews did not begin following Christ until well after the resurrection.

All the same, to the question "What religion was Jesus?" uninformed people often respond, "Christian" (with "Well, duh," levels of incredulity at the asking). That's why it's important first and foremost to highlight that Jesus and his disciples were not Christians pushing back against unbelievers but faithful Jews, following teaching, preaching, healing, and worship traditions going back into Jewish history; and their adversaries were not "the Jews," but other Jewish characters in the story who understood the revelation of God and Jesus's presence in a very different way. Some scholars and pastors would like to see the Greek word *ioudaios* (which is usually translated as "the Jews") rendered as "the Judeans" or even "the leaders" to reflect a better understanding of those other Jewish characters who oppose Jesus and his followers, but however we translate the Greek, it's essential that we have a context for why the Gospel of John villainizes and even demonizes these characters.

When we find "the Jews" doing this or "the Jews" saying that or Jewish characters expressing "fear of the Jews" (as happens often in the Gospel of John), we need to understand some possible reasons that "the Jews" in John's Gospel might be presented as villains in a narrative made up mostly of Jews, since we have a responsibility to push back against false understandings that have led to Gentiles fearing, hating, and hurting Jews.

One of the often-repeated understandings of the early Christian community that formed around the Gospel of John as their distinctive recording of the story of Jesus and call to faith is that these proto-Christians were Jews rejected by the synagogue (the local Jewish house of prayer, reading, assembly) because of their views about who and what Jesus was.

The great biblical scholar N. T. Wright has described this battle as being not between people who barely know or understand each other, but as a family fight, a dispute between people who have lived with and have loved each other. As we all know, a disagreement in the family can be the most painful kind of conflict, and there are two possible responses, as you may remember from your last argument around the Thanksgiving table: you can decide to remain in contact and engaged in conversation despite your disagreements, or you can distance yourself from those family members with whom you disagree—cast them out of your head and out of your life (or try to). It is this second tack that the synagogue seems to have taken with the community that formed around John's Gospel, and vice versa, and this is an essential understanding for all Christians reading John today.

Being misunderstood or rejected by the people we have loved can lead us to villainize them. If your sister can't accept you because you're gay, for example, it's a short step to calling her a self-righteous bigot, even if she may have reasons for the choice she's making. Pain and shame and imperfect understanding—particularly where we expect the opposite—can be too painful to bear, so we see the community that gathered around the Gospel of John lashing out against the community that pushed them away, even though they themselves identify as members of the group.

They even demonize the family members who have rejected them, calling their humanity into question. Elaine Pagels, in her book *The Origin of Satan,* helps us understand how the supernatural figure of Satan figures into this story. Only supernatural evil could account for the way people who should love us have treated us, for their failure to understand the truth as we understand it, and so Satan becomes a character in the story lined up in opposition to the faithful followers on the other side.

In the eighth chapter of John, we find Jesus speaking to a large group of Jews divided between those who believe in him as the Messiah and those who do not, and in the heat of his own anger, he says to the latter group that they are not children of Abraham:

> "You are from your father the devil, and you choose to do your father's desires. He was a murderer from the beginning and does not stand in the truth, because there is no truth in him. When he lies, he speaks according to his own nature, for he is a liar and the father of lies. But because I tell the truth, you do not believe me." (John 8:44–45 NRSV)

Abraham Lincoln, in his First Inaugural Address, anticipated another bitter family conflict, the American Civil War. "We are not enemies," he said,

> but friends. We must not be enemies. Though passion may have strained, it must not break our bonds of affec-

tion. The mystic chords of memory, stretching from every battle-field, and patriot grave, to every living heart and hearthstone, all over this broad land, will yet swell the chorus of the Union, when again touched, as surely they will be, by the better angels of our nature.

As the years have turned into centuries, Christians have sometimes forgotten that this is a family squabble, have denied the common bonds of our affection, have ignored the better angels of our nature, have turned instead to diabolical explanations. It's okay for me to criticize my family, but the tragic irony is that misunderstanding that this is a family squabble has led some Christians to demonize and reject all Jews, to take Jesus's angry rejoinders and consider them to be existential truths. As Christians have forgotten or foresworn our own family relationship with Judaism, they have often ignored or even lost the debt we owe to "the Jews."

The Christian Testament is stacked with examples of that common heritage. In the Gospel of Luke, Jesus initiates his public ministry by reading from the scroll of the prophet Isaiah (Christians often forget that the "Bible" Jesus read was the Hebrew Scriptures, and ignore his very real debt to the prophets). In that Gospel, after Jesus rolls up the scroll, he says, in effect, this is why I am here. What God revealed to Isaiah is what God is bringing about now through me.

The writer of the Gospel of Matthew introduces Jesus as the inheritor of a long line of promises made to faithful Jews stretching back generations and generations. It's why Matthew begins with a genealogy and not with a nativity scene. Jesus is a descendant of the great King David. Of Abraham. Of strong and surprising women in the history of the Jews. It's what I love, in fact, about my friend Lauren Winner's rendering of Matthew for our contemporary Bible translation *The Voice*, which foregrounds the amazing women in Jesus's genealogy and in our own salvation history.[1]

But when we forget those debts and our common heritage,

---

1. *The Voice* (Nashville: Thomas Nelson, 2012).

when we dwell only on the cultural and religious differences between Jews and Christians, it can lead to fear. Fear grows out of prejudice, out of unfamiliarity, out of distance, and fear is, in many ways, the most dangerous human emotion because it alters our decision-making process for the worse. Thomas Aquinas, the great Catholic theologian, talked about appropriate fear, about reacting properly to threats that might not be life threatening but that nonetheless get our hearts racing.

Out of that fear, we often make narrow, closed-off decisions that can lead to violence or rejection. The ethicist Scott Bader-Saye has written beautifully about what happens when we react to events and decisions primarily through the filter of fear: when I am afraid, my security (and that of those around me) becomes my primary criterion for choice. Not love, not respect, not compassion, not hospitality. Security. My world contracts to a finite set of options.[2]

And my fear can so easily become hate, can become my unwillingness to recognize our common humanity, let alone that family resemblance. It can become bigotry, leading me to obsess over our differences and seeing the other as inferior to me and my way of being.

Differences in belief, or appearance, or behavior can be interpreted as signs that those we hate and fear are not human as we are human, can turn into the infamous blood libel of the Middle Ages (preposterous defamations that Jews employed the blood of Christians in religious rituals), can induce us to label Jews "Christ killers," to think of Jews as vermin, to persecute and prosecute and expel them, as indeed did happen in many Western nations over the past one thousand years.

It can move us from seeing them as our brothers and sisters in the Abrahamic tradition or even as fellow members of the human family to trying to prevent them from practicing their faith, from working in their chosen professions, from living and breathing free, as every child of God deserves.

---

2. Scott Bader-Saye, *Following Jesus in a Culture of Fear* (Grand Rapids, MI: Brazos, 2007).

Hitler's Final Solution stands as the most brutal and most fatal manifestation of antisemitism, but it is hardly a great achievement to say, "Well, at least we didn't go that far." America differs from that horror by degrees, but our hands are far from clean. America did not intervene in that Final Solution, even after our government learned what Hitler was doing. The Ku Klux Klan has never limited its hatred to blacks, but included Jews as well, while the Neo-Nazis marching in Charlottesville, Virginia, chanted, "The Jews will not replace us," among other hateful things. Even without including our own ultimate horror of recent synagogue shootings, Americans have a long painful history of antisemitism; and often Christians and our readings of the Christian Testament have been the engine of this prejudice.

Even today, when evangelical Christians seem to champion the Jews and encourage the world to recognize Jerusalem as Israel's capital, it is important to observe that this strongly held belief is less about solidarity with the Jews and more about bringing about these Christians' version of the Second Coming of Jesus, which cannot happen, they think, until a set of circumstances are fulfilled in the Holy Land. This belief is the ultimate supersessionist move; Christians have the true scoop about the end of the world and how God is moving in it, and the Jews are merely expendable pawns in their game.

When Jews are not equal partners in our narrative, when they are only supporting characters in the story in which we live, we can make whatever use of them we want. When we don't know them, love them, value them, they are puppets, stick figures who don't need to be treated as fully human.

I know something about this. I grew up in a tradition that spoke of the Christ-killing Jews, in a tradition whose leaders opined that God did not hear the prayers of a faithful Jew. There was no synagogue in the small town where I went to high school, no Jew in our school.

That is why I am so thankful that my daughters attend truly diverse schools in a part of Austin, Texas, inhabited by Christians, Buddhists, Muslim, Hindus, and Jews. We live only a few blocks away from the Dell Jewish Community Center, and are members at the JCC. We sweat in the gym alongside observant and cultural Jews. Our daughters go to camps, play volleyball, swim, and practice gymnastics at the J, which also hosts the campuses of Congregation Tiferet Israel (Orthodox), Congregation Agudas Achim (Conservative), and Temple Beth Shalom (Reform).

This close proximity has enlarged our understanding and our sympathy, and instead of fear *of* the Jews, what has grown in me is fear *for* the Jews. In the wake of the violent racism and antisemitism that has grown since the 2016 general elections, I discover that I have begun to identify my Jewish acquaintances not just as fellow members of the human family but as friends facing a looming threat. I've also come to feel powerful guilt for the way they have been treated by people like those with whom I grew up who call themselves Christian. On the Saturday of the Pittsburgh shooting, as I was driving home from the J, I saw an Orthodox family walking home from Congregation Tiferet Israel, and I pulled over and told them, tears in my eyes, "I am so sorry."

Does this mean anything? Is my expression of sympathy in any way meaningful, coming as it does from those who have historically persecuted the Jews? I believe it does, and could be emblematic of something much larger than my individual act. In the Christian tradition, we speak about contrition, about how our process of change should include our sorrow, our expression of regret, and our intention to change.

Perhaps we personally have not been violent or hateful. But perhaps we have stood by silent when violence and hate took place. Perhaps we have said, "They're not members of my family." Perhaps we have stood in a pulpit on Sunday morning and failed to push back against antisemitism in our Holy Scriptures. Maya Angelou, of blessed memory, used to ceaselessly quote the Latin writer Terence: "I am human, therefore nothing human can be alien to me." At the very least—and this is a very low bar for those who profess to follow Christ—every human being deserves our sympathy and empathy because they are just like us.

But I would argue that there is much more we need to do to even the scales of history, to push back against a racist and anti-semitic tide. We need to acknowledge our family resemblance. We pray to the same God, profess the same ethical teachings, revere the same prophets. There are differences in the way we live out our faith, but that difference does not have to lead to fear.

We should defend our Jewish brothers and sisters from harm, yes, but also defend them from calumny, even when that calumny comes from our own Christian Testament, because slander leads to fear, which leads to hatred, which leads to violence.

CHAPTER 14

What Do We Say to Our Children?

RABBI SANDY EISENBERG SASSO

Children are endowed with an innate spirituality. What they don't always have is the language to express it. As parents, educators, and clergy we can help them develop the language and provide the tools to reflect and explore their spiritual experiences in ways that affirm their religious traditions while appreciating and respecting others.

For children, religious language must be accessible, rich in images, concrete (connected to their world), and open to conversation. Often, we begin with the opposite: obscure, abstract, ethereal, and closed to questions. We mistakenly believe that children are not ready for theological talk, and we ignore that conversation at our own peril, leading children to either reject belief as childish fantasy (just as they outgrow Santa Claus), or reject others who do not adhere to their religion.

We assume that belief is something we have and children don't, so we have to give it to them. We offer them faith from the outside, rather than help them to discover it within. In order to cement religious identity, we teach children that their faith community and its understanding of God are better and superior to any other, an exclusive theology that inevitably leads to intolerance. A prime example is the teaching that the New Testament ("new covenant") comes to displace and supplant the Old Testament ("old covenant"). The new (Christianity) is presented as better, more advanced, more enlightened than the old (Judaism).

We all use categories of people, places, and things to make sense of the world around us. For example, we subsume all types of drinking vessels under the word "cup." That word is used to include a mug, tumbler, chalice, or a crystal glass. Categorization becomes stereotyping when we add cultural presumptions. For example, cups are mundane. Stereotyping becomes prejudice when we add the belief that a category's characteristics are superior to another's. For instance, cups are less beautiful than crystal glasses, less sacred than chalices. What is true for groups of cups is true for religious groups.

The category of "Jew" is used to speak of those people who adhere to Judaism. There is no distinction among observant, nonobservant, or secular Jews, or between American, Middle Eastern, or European Jews, black or Hispanic Jews. This categorization becomes stereotyping when we say that Jews focus on "Law," a mistranslation of Torah, which means "teaching." Then the stereotype turns to prejudice when that "law" is said to be opposed to "compassion," the latter being deemed superior to the former.

The New Testament is often read and preached over and against Judaism. Jesus is identified with forgiveness and love, while the Pharisees and the rabbinic teachers who shaped the foundations of Judaism two millennia ago are identified with strict justice and rules. This is a misrepresentation of Judaism and a source of bigotry.

Thus the following is such an interpretation of the parable of the Prodigal Son (Luke 15:17–20):

> The eldest son represents the Jewish leaders. The religious leaders saw their rewards due for their works. They didn't understand that they can bring nothing to the plan of salvation and if they try to earn it, they do not understand how God saves and that it is Jesus' righteousness alone that accounts them worthy. (stjohnsbloomington.org)

It is my understanding, from Christian friends and colleagues, that this interpretation is quite representative of what is heard in churches throughout the United States.

Here Jesus is presented as different from and wiser than the Jewish leaders of his time. The implication is that the God of Christianity is kinder and more forgiving than the God of Judaism. Christianity and Jesus are presented as compassionate, and loving. Judaism and its teachers (even though, of course, Jesus was a Jewish teacher) are presented as stern, legalistic, and heartless. When children hear such lessons in Sunday School classes and from the pulpit, they develop wrong and harmful attitudes toward Jews that often turn into unconscious prejudices.

One online site, "Ministry to Children," says the following about the Old Testament:

> Back when He (Jesus) was on earth they didn't have the New Testament yet, but they did have the Old Testament. And do you know what the Old Testament is full of? Rules. . . . There was so much time spent learning and following laws and tradition that many people forgot the most important law of all. To love God.

Again, this site, and this view, is representative of what might be called mainstream Christian teaching today. In other words, I am not selecting examples from people who are intending to be hateful. (Those examples are far, far worse.)

But this teaching misses the point that in Jesus's time there was no Christianity. Jesus spoke out of his grounding in Judaism, and his teaching of love of God and love of neighbor are core Jewish religious values. Do we forget these things, or is it simply easier to overlook them? Jesus quoted Jewish Scripture when he said, "Love your neighbor as yourself" (Leviticus 19:18), and "Love the Lord your God with all your heart and all your might" (Deuteronomy 6:5).

Knowing that Hillel, a Jewish sage of the first century BCE, taught "What is hateful to you, do not do to your neighbor" helps children recognize that the Golden Rule is an integral part of Judaism and not a Christian innovation. Another Jewish leader, Rabbi Akiba, taught that "Love your neighbor as yourself" was the most important teaching of the Torah. To present

Christianity as a tradition of love and grace and Judaism as a religion of rules and righteousness is incorrect and potentially dangerous.

Another Sunday School online site (https://ministry-to-children.com/bible-layout-lesson-two) says that the purpose of teaching the organization of the Old Testament is to show how each section of books points to Christ. Using the Hebrew Bible primarily as a Christian referent is historically inaccurate and misappropriates Jewish Scripture.

What Christians often call the Old Testament is called *TaNaKh* in Hebrew. The name is an acronym for the tripartite division of the Hebrew Bible: Torah (Teaching), Neviim (Prophets), and Ketuvim (Writings). The Hebrew Bible has its own integrity independently of the New Testament. Jews interpret the *TaNaKh* through the teachings of the rabbis in the first centuries of the Common Era in literature called the Midrash and the Talmud. These writings form the foundation of Jewish life in the synagogue and home. Christians interpret the "Old Testament" through the New Testament and the teachings of the early church fathers. Those interpretations form the foundation of the church. Suggesting that all the books of the Hebrew Bible point to Christ implies that only Christians have the correct understanding of Scripture and Jews are wrong.

Negative views of the Pharisees are also problematic, and rampant in stories in Christian children's Bibles. The Pharisees are depicted as overly legalistic, hypocrites, and the foil against Jesus's teaching of humility, forgiveness, and compassion. As Christianity was separating itself from Judaism, the church created a caricature of the Jewish leaders of the time, and the Pharisees became the villains. Derogatory statements about Pharisees are pervasive and quickly turn into offensive views of the Jews.

One well-intended approach to counter prejudice has been to deny and avoid discussing differences altogether—we are all the same after all. But racial, cultural, and religious differences exist. We can see them. Children see them. When we focus on the ways we are the same and are silent about differences, children may conclude that differences are bad and we shouldn't discuss them.

Differences become prejudices when turned into stereotypes and labeled as inferior or superior. Adults need to help children make sense of diversity in ways that are honest and do not degrade or denigrate another group of people. They need to tell their stories not as over and against the other but as equally authentic.

Teaching early Christian stories as embedded in the Judaism of their time rather than as antagonistic to the Jewish tradition out of which they grew offers not only a more sympathetic view of Jews but a more accurate understanding of Jesus. Recognizing how Judaism and Christianity share common teachings yet have genuine differences of belief and practice helps Christian and other children not just tolerate Jews but appreciate and respect their teachings and their contributions to the wisdom of Jesus.

Jesus taught, "If you are offering your gift at the altar and remember that your brother has something against you, leave your gift in front of the altar. First go and be reconciled to your brother—then come and offer your gift" (Matthew 5:23–24). Too much misrepresentation over the centuries has supported hatred and mistrust. It is time for brothers and sisters to be reconciled to one another. Their gifts will be richer for all.

"If not now, when?"
(Hillel, Pirke Avot 1:14)

AMY-JILL LEVINE

The essays in this volume address what has been called the "Longest Hatred."[1] More than seventy years from the liberation of the Nazi death camps and more than fifty years from the promulgation of the conciliar document *Nostra Aetate*, this hatred continues. There are multiple reasons, not all of them religious: the racist view that Jews are genetically inferior or inherently deceitful and misanthropic; the political claims that Jews control the banks and the media, or have dual loyalties, or are behind the immigrant caravans into the United States. The Charlottesville contingent who claimed "Jews will not replace us" were not prompted, primarily, by reading the New Testament or from hearing a Sunday homily.

Yet we cannot exculpate the Christian Bible and its readers either. These nonreligious lies often find their roots, or at least their fertilizers, in Scripture, whether in Matthew's murderous Pharisees (23:35), John's claim that "the Jews" are "children of the devil" (8:44), Luke's insistence that Pharisees are "lovers of money" (16:14), Paul's notice (1 Thessalonians 2:14b) of the "Jews who killed the Lord Jesus," or any of the other texts

---

1. Robert Solomon Wistrich, *Antisemitism: The Longest Hatred* (New York: Schocken Books, 1994).

that portray Jews negatively. The essays in this volume, from historical reporting to personal reflection, church proclamation to children's education, open points for conversation, which is what good books should do.

There are several ways to continue rather than to foreclose such conversation. The first is to do what this book does: acknowledge scriptural prompts for anti-Jewish readings. When I point out difficult passages, I frequently hear in response, "What about holy war in the Old Testament?" or "The Talmud says bad things about Jesus." Such responses, which are factually correct if not equivalent in impact over the past two thousand years, preclude conversation rather than promote correction. We can take a cue here from #BlackLivesMatter. All groups have baggage, and all people have sin: the task *here* is to address Jew-hatred rather than deflect the charge, as white people might do in denying their privilege or responding with fragility.[2] We need to clean our own houses rather than to excuse the dirt or seek to besmirch others.

Second, we need to talk about vocabulary, and here discussion between Jews and Christians—the best way of doing Jewish/Christian relations—is needed. For example, while the term "Hebrew Bible" rather than "Old Testament" can eliminate the potentially negative impression of "old," I find it neither accurate nor helpful. Some of that text is not in Hebrew but in Aramaic; moreover, the "Old Testament" of the Catholic, Anglican, and Orthodox Churches has Greek material. "Hebrew Bible" also elides the distinctions in the order of the books between the church's Old Testament and the synagogue's *Tanakh*. Nor is "Christian Testament" helpful for the second part of the church's canon, because it suggests that the first part is not part of the Christian canon as well. "Old Testament" is better, as in "old time rock and roll," for the first part of the Christian canon,

---

2. See Amy-Jill Levine, "Christian Privilege, Christian Fragility, and the Gospel of John," in Adele Reinhartz (ed.), *The Gospel of John and Jewish-Christian Relations* (Lanham, MD: Lexington/Fortress, 2018), 87–110.

for that "old" is something that can soothe the soul.[3] For the Jewish Scriptures, the term *Tanakh* is appropriate.[4]

Third, on what to call those *Ioudaioi* who, according to John, are "children of the devil" and, according to Paul, "killed the Lord Jesus," again we have options. Although "Judean" is a plausible translation, I find it both literarily awkward and historically unfaithful. On the literary side, John uses the term seventy-one times, and readers will not stop to ask, "Which group does he mean here?" Moreover, in John's Gospel, Jesus is not a Judean; he is Galilean. Neo-Nazi and KKK websites promote the "Judean" translation because it can suggest, despite the good intentions of those who use it to eliminate anti-Jewish proclamation, both that there are no "Jews" in the New Testament and that Jesus was not a Jew.[5] "Judean" also eliminates the connections between Jews in the first century and Jews today. If we want to see Jesus as a Jew—as we should—we need the word "Jews" in the New Testament. And if we want to confront the problem, changing the words will not help.

Related is the question of continuity among Israelites, Judahites, Yehudim, Judeans, and Jews. Sweeney insists, "Judaism today bears almost no resemblance to the faith and practices of the ancient Israelites." Yes, and no. While reading Leviticus does not tell us what Jews do in local synagogues, Jewish tradition claims unbroken continuity. The Mishnah *Pirke Avot*

---

3. Paraphrase of a lyric from "Old Time Rock N Roll," by George Jackson and Thomas E. Jones III; recorded by Bob Seger in his 1978 album, *Stranger in Town*.

4. On terminology, see Amy-Jill Levine, "What is the Difference between the Old Testament, the Tanakh, and the Hebrew Bible," n.p., https://www.bible odyssey.org:443/tools/bible-basics/what-is-the-difference-between-the-old-testament-the-tanakh-and-the-hebrew-bible.

5. See Amy-Jill Levine, *The Misunderstood Jew: The Church and the Scandal of the Jewish Jesus* (New York: HarperOne, 2004), 159–60; Adele Reinhartz, "The Vanishing Jews of Antiquity," in *Jew and Judean: A Marginalia Forum on Politics and Historiography in the Translation of Ancient Texts,* ed. Timothy Michael Law and Charles Halton, *Marginalia | Los Angeles Review of Books* (June 24, 2014): 10–23.

begins, "Moses received Torah at Sinai and delivered it to Joshua, Joshua to the elders, and elders to prophets, and prophets delivered it to the men of the Great Assembly" and then to Simeon the Righteous, Hillel and Shammai, Rabban Gamaliel son of Rabbi Judah the Patriarch, and so on. From antiquity to the present, Jews traditionally claim a connection to the land of Israel, honor the Sabbath, attend to what we eat and wear, and promote love of God, neighbor, and stranger. Abraham was not a "Jew" in the sense of someone who lived in Judea or practiced something called "Judaism" (he knew neither term), but Jews recognize him as the first Jew.

Christians similarly self-identify as heirs to the assemblies in Thessalonica and Rome, but those ancient believers were not reciting the Nicene Creed, had no organ or hymnal, and lacked a "New Testament." Paul did not call himself a "Christian"; he did not know the term. We need to know our pasts as well as how we relate to and differ from them in practice and belief.

Fourth is the fraught question of Israel/Palestine. Numerous Christians have asked me why "Jews continue to persecute the Palestinians." The question presumes incorrectly that all Jews think alike, that "Jew" and "Israeli" are equivalent, and that the present situation is entirely Israel's fault. I want to say "amen" to the numerous Christian initiatives for pulling back Israeli settlements "built in territory conquered by Israel in the Six Day War (June 1967),"[6] and establishing a Palestinian state. I sometimes cannot do so, for their well-intended efforts often bleed into antisemitic rhetoric. Here we do well to listen to how our words sound in another's ears.

How do we prevent using biblical material as "the ideological tool of preference and privilege that serves exploitative self-interest (as in the case of West Bank 'settlers')" (so Brueggemann) *and at the same time* prevent using the same text as a supersessionist screed that denies Jews a homeland and sees the promises to the people Israel as transferred to Christians

---

6. Definition from and discussion in Americans for Peace Now, "Settlements 101 (7/07/10) at https://peacenow.org/entry.php?id=6198#.XUr5ui3Mxp9.

(as is the case with some Christian "Palestinianists")? Supersessionism is alive and well in pockets of Christian anti-Zionism. Jewish self-determination in Israel and Palestinian self-determination in Palestine are both worthy goals; both parties have attempted to gain those goals in horrific ways; both have used the Bible (or, for some Palestinians, the Qur'an and Hadith) to make their case. All texts can be deployed to support prejudice; all people should be on their guard to prevent it.

Next, we do well to locate the misperceptions. Here, Mary Boys's "typical rendition of Christian origins" is spot on. We can also dig more deeply into the conventional claims that appear to be more respectful of Jewish tradition.

Conventional wisdom suggests that John is writing to a group of Jews excommunicated from the synagogue. However, we have no examples of such excommunication from antiquity; to the contrary, Paul is disciplined from within the synagogue system, and centuries later, John Chrysostom complains about church members attending synagogue programs. The analogy to Martin Luther and the Catholic Church is not helpful, for it presumes that there was something so dreadfully wrong with Judaism that a new movement was required. Nor do we actually have a "Johannine community" or a "Matthean community"; a text is not a community. We have texts, distributed and copied across the Gentile Christian world.[7] Presuming that John's rhetoric is reactive places the blame for it ultimately on "the Jews" who expelled Jesus followers.

Conventional wisdom suggests that Paul persecuted Jesus's followers because he found their theology heretical. That is not what Paul tells us, and the claim is historically unlikely. First-century Jews had a variety of theological beliefs and messianic expectations. Were Paul's issue theological, he could have stayed in Jerusalem and harassed Peter and James. He does not. He heads to Damascus because Jewish Christ-followers were telling *Gentiles* to stop worshiping state gods, stop eating meat

---

7. See Adele Reinhartz, *Cast Out of the Covenant: Jews and Anti-Judaism in the Gospel of John* (Philadelphia: Lexington Books/Fortress Academic, 2018).

offered to idols, stop participating in their parents' rituals, and instead worship the God of the Jews and his son, put to death by the empire. That is, they were putting lives of other Jews, whether Christ-followers or not, in danger.

Conventional wisdom tells us that the writers of the New Testament books were Jews. Paul was a "Hebrew born of Hebrews" (Philippians 3:5). I suspect the authors of Matthew and John, James and Revelation also come from within the Jewish tradition. But the jury is out on the other authors, such as the evangelists known as Mark and Luke, and the composers of the Pastoral and Petrine Epistles as well as of Hebrews. That authors look to the "Old Testament" to understand Jesus does *not* tell us that these authors are Jews, any more than a Catholic or Presbyterian who looks to Genesis or Jeremiah for instruction is a Jew. Nor again would a Jew be incapable of anti-Jewish commentary, just as Americans can be guilty of anti-American activities (variously defined) or a Christian can be guilty of heresy (again, variously defined). Old Testament roots can, with appropriate grafts, produce Gentile branches.

I am also doubtful that all New Testament invective reflects sibling rivalry. The vituperation of the Dead Sea Scrolls differs from that of the New Testament, in that the scrolls are written to and about fellow Jews, but the New Testament texts are addressed not just to Jews but primarily *to Gentiles*.

The most important question may be Sandy Sasso's "What do we say to our children?" Bigotry begins with the well-meaning Sunday School or Vacation Bible School teacher who repeats conventional wisdom: the Jews think of Law rather than Love, the Jews are hypocrites, the Jews killed Jesus, Jews are offering animal sacrifices, Jews use Christian blood to bake matzoh, and so on. These are not hypotheticals; my students have heard all these libels, and more, from their well-meaning but misguided teachers. It begins when children in the congregation hear the Sunday lectionary reading, and the lesson—the take-away from the simple reading of the text—can easily be "Thank God we're not like those hypocritical, money-loving, murderous, legalistic Jews." We can do better.

Better would be to face the textual problems rather than to explain them (away) by hypothetical historical contextualization.

Better would be to have church groups move from general statements to providing *specific* guidance to pastors and priests on addressing the problematic texts and to fixing the lectionary where it gives a supersessionist impression.

Better would be for church bodies to insist that candidates for ordained ministry learn about Second Temple and Rabbinic Judaism so that they do not bear false witness against Jews and Judaism.

Better would be for anyone who proclaims this text to picture Jewish children in the front pew.

To do this work, we need to listen to how texts sound in the ears of our neighbors. We need to develop midrashim for reinterpretation. And we need to move, finally, from yet another general proclamation and yet another volume on why there is yet another attack on Jews, and do more in seminary education, requirements for ordination, liturgical readings, children and adult education, and interreligious studies.

About the Contributors

MARY C. BOYS, SNJM, is Skinner and McAlpin Professor of Practical Theology at Union Theological Seminary in the City of New York. She was the recipient in 2005 of the Sternberg Award from the International Council of Christians and Jews, of the Eternal Light Award from St. Leo College in 2012, the Ann O'Hara Graf Memorial Award from the Catholic Theological Society of America in 2013, and of the *Nostra Aetate* Award from Seton Hall University in 2015. Professor Boys is a member of the Committee on Religion, Ethics, and the Holocaust at the U.S. Holocaust Memorial Museum in Washington, DC, and the National Catholic Center for Holocaust Education at Seton Hall University. Formerly, she served on the board of the Catholic Theological Society of America and on the advisory committee for the Secretariat for Ecumenical and Interreligious Affairs of the United States Conference of Catholic Bishops. She is the author of many books, including *Redeeming Our Sacred Story: The Death of Jesus and Relations between Jews and Christians*; and *Christians and Jews in Dialogue: Learning in the Presence of the Other*.

WES HOWARD-BROOK was raised Jewish and claims the Way of the Jewish Jesus. He teaches Bible and theology at Seattle University and partners in the ministry Abide in Me with his wife, spiritual director Sue Ferguson Johnson. He is the author, coauthor, or coeditor of many books, including *Becoming Children of God: John's Gospel and Radical Discipleship*; *The Church before Christianity*; and *John's Gospel and the Renewal of the Church*.

WALTER BRUEGGEMANN is William Marcellus McPheeters Professor of Old Testament Emeritus at Columbia Theological Seminary, where he taught from 1986 to 2003. He was a professor at Eden Seminary in St. Louis from 1961 to 1986. He earned his ThD from Union Theological Seminary in New York, and a PhD from Saint Louis University. He is also an ordained minister in the United Church of Christ. Brueggemann is considered one of the world's leading interpreters of the Hebrew Bible and is the author of numerous books, including *Hopeful Imagination: Prophetic Voices in Exile*; *The Prophetic Imagination*; *An Introduction to the Old Testament: The Canon and Christian Imagination*; and *Reverberations of Faith: A Theological Handbook of Old Testament Themes*.

ROBERT ELLSBERG is the publisher of Orbis Books and the author of many books, including *All Saints: Daily Reflections on Saints, Prophets, and Witnesses for Our Time*; *Blessed among Us*; and *A Living Gospel: Reading God's Story in Holy Lives*. He has edited the writings of Dorothy Day, as well as of Pope Francis, including *A Stranger and You Welcomed Me: A Call to Mercy and Solidarity with Migrants and Refugees*.

MASSIMO FAGGIOLI is one of the leading authorities on the history and administrative inner workings of the Catholic Church with specific expertise in the papacy, Vatican II, the Roman Curia, liturgical reform, new Catholic movements, and Catholicism and global politics. Frequently featured in national and international electronic and print media, Faggioli is also a professor of theology and religious studies at Villanova University, Philadelphia, and a contributing writer to *Commonweal* magazine. He received his PhD in religious history from the University of Turin (Italy) in 2002. His books and articles have been published in eight languages. Recent books include *Vatican II: The Battle for Meaning*; *Pope Francis: Tradition in Transition*; *A Council for the Global Church: Receiving Vatican II in History*; and *The Rising Laity: Ecclesial Movements since Vatican II*.

GREG GARRETT is best known for his writings on faith, culture, race, politics, and narrative. BBC Radio has called Greg "one of America's leading voices on religion and culture." His most recent nonfiction books are *In Conversation: Rowan Williams and Greg Garrett*; *Living with the Living Dead: The Wisdom of the Zombie Apocalypse*; *Crossing Myself: A Story of Spiritual Rebirth*; and *Entertaining Judgment: The Afterlife in Literature and Culture.* His books have been translated into five languages. He has also written hundreds of articles and essays for *Salon*, *The Washington Post*, *The Tablet* (UK), *Christianity Today*, *Reform* (UK), *The Spectator* (UK), and many other publications. His book on race and American culture, *A Long, Long Way*, will be published by Oxford University Press in June 2020. Greg is an award-winning professor of English at Baylor University (Texas); Theologian in Residence at the American Cathedral in Paris; and an elected member of the Texas Institute of Letters.

NICHOLAS ("NICK") KING, SJ, is a Jesuit of the British Province. He was educated at Stonyhurst, and then read Greats ("Classics") at St. John's College, Oxford, after which he entered the Society of Jesus. He studied philosophy and theology at Heythrop College in the University of London, then taught for a year. After that he returned to Oxford to do an MPhil in early Judaism at the Oriental Institute. Then he was ordained and taught for two years at Heythrop, and two years at St. Aloysius College, Glasgow. After his Jesuit tertianship in Spokane, Washington, he taught at Stonyhurst for four years, before moving to South Africa to teach New Testament and moral philosophy in various seminaries and universities. One of the greatest days of King's life was in April 1994, when he was able to serve as a district observer during the first democratic elections in that country. He returned to the United Kingdom in 2001, and has been teaching New Testament and related languages at Campion Hall, Oxford, ever since.

AMY-JILL LEVINE is University Professor of New Testament and Jewish Studies and Mary Jane Werthan Professor of Jewish Studies at Vanderbilt Divinity School and Program in Jewish Studies. An internationally renowned scholar and teacher, she has written and edited more than thirty books including *The*

Misunderstood Jew: The Church and the Scandal of the Jewish Jesus; *Short Stories by Jesus: The Enigmatic Parables of a Controversial Rabbi*; four children's books (with Sandy Sasso); *The Gospel of Luke* (with Ben Witherington III—the first biblical commentary authored by a Jew and an Evangelical Protestant); and *The Jewish Annotated New Testament* (co-edited with Marc Z. Brettler). For Abingdon Press, she has produced three adult-education Bible studies (on Jesus's parables, the Passion Narrative, and the Christmas stories). In 2019 she became the first Jew to teach a course on the New Testament at Rome's Pontifical Biblical Institute. She has given over five hundred presentations to churches, synagogues, and academic audiences.

RICHARD C. LUX is Professor Emeritus of Scripture Studies at Sacred Heart Seminary and School of Theology (Hales Corners, Wisconsin), and founding director of The Lux Center for Catholic–Jewish Studies, there. He earned his PhD from the University of Notre Dame. Lux's teaching, public lectures, travel, publications, and energetic personal outreach have brought rich perspectives on Judaism and Israel to thousands of students, researchers, religious leaders, and laity for more than five decades. He is the author of *The Jewish People, the Holy Land, and the State of Israel: A Catholic View*.

RABBI SANDY EISENBERG SASSO is currently the Director of Religion, Spirituality, and the Arts at IUPUI Arts and Humanities. She was the second woman to be ordained as a rabbi (1974) and the first rabbi in the world to become a mother. She and her husband, Dennis, were also the first rabbinical couple to jointly lead a congregation—Beth-El Zedeck in Indianapolis. She earned a Doctorate of Ministry from Christian Theological Seminary and is the author of many acclaimed children's books including *God's Paintbrush*; *In God's Name*; and *The Story of And: The Little Word That Changed the World*. With Amy-Jill Levine she has written *Who Counts? 100 Sheep, 10 Coins, and 2 Sons*; *The Marvelous Mustard Seed*; and *Who Is My Neighbor?*, also for children, parents, and teachers of the Bible. Rabbi Sandy's books for older readers include *Midrash: Reading the Bible with Question Marks.*

THE MOST REVEREND RICHARD J. SKLBA is Auxiliary Bishop Emeritus of Milwaukee, Wisconsin. For thirty years, Bishop Sklba served on various committees of the U.S. Conference of Catholic Bishops including Priestly Life and Ministry, Doctrine, Liturgy, Permanent Diaconate, and Marriage and Family. He was appointed to task forces including the Teaching Function of the Diocesan Bishop and the subcommittee for Inclusive Language. He chaired the subcommittee on the Review of Scripture Translations from 1991 to 2001. Bishop Sklba served as chair of the USCCB's Committee for Ecumenical and Interreligious Affairs from 2005 to 2008. In that capacity, he had the privilege of introducing the nation's religious leaders from several traditions including Jewish, Islamic, Buddhist, Hindu, and Jain to Pope Benedict XVI during the Holy Father's historic pastoral visit to the United States in April of 2008. He has been a member of the Catholic Biblical Association of America since 1968 and served as its president in 1982. Over the years, he also participated in several archaeological expeditions to sites in Israel. Active in the Catholic Church's ecumenical and interreligious relationships on a national and local level, Bishop Sklba was invited to attend the ninth General Assembly of the World Council of Churches in Porto Alegre, Brazil, as a member of the official Vatican delegation headed by Cardinal Walter Kasper. He has been an invited ecumenical guest at many national meetings of the country's mainline Protestant churches. He has also participated in countless meetings and projects with Jewish scholars of the country to promote interreligious understanding and cooperation. He also taught Scripture at Sacred Heart School of Theology, Hales Corners, Wisconsin, from 2006 to 2009.

RABBI ABRAHAM SKORKA was born in Buenos Aires. He earned a PhD in chemistry from the University of Buenos Aires, and graduated from Midrahsa HaIvrit and the Latin-American

Rabbinical Seminary. He was the rabbi of Benei Tikva synagogue for forty-two years and rector of the Rabbinical Seminary for twenty years. He has published many articles and books, including *On Heaven and Earth*, an international bestseller, which he wrote with then-Archbishop of Buenos Aires, Cardinal Bergoglio, who is now Pope Francis. Rabbi Skorka has received honorary doctorates from the Pontifical Catholic University of Argentina, Jewish Theological Seminary, and Sacred Heart University. He has received awards from the legislature of the Autonomous City of Buenos Aires, the Polish Council of Christians and Jews, The Eternal Light Award from St. Leo University Center for Catholic and Jewish Understanding, and The Jan Karski Eagle Award. He is currently University Professor at Saint Joseph's University in Philadelphia, working closely with its Institute for Jewish-Catholic Relations.

JON M. SWEENEY is an award-winning author who has been interviewed by a wide range of publications from the *Dallas Morning News* and the *LA Times* to *The Irish Catholic* and the *CBC*, on television for CBS Saturday Morning, Fox News, CBS-TV Chicago, Religion and Ethics Newsweekly, and public television's Chicago Tonight. His history, *The Pope Who Quit*, was optioned by HBO. He's the author of more than thirty books, including *The Complete Francis of Assisi*; *The Pope's Cat* fiction series for children; *Meister Eckhart's Book of the Heart*, with Mark S. Burrows; *St. Francis of Assisi: His Life, Teachings, and Practice*, with a foreword by Richard Rohr; and a biography, *James Martin, SJ: In the Company of Jesus*. He is a Catholic, married to a rabbi; their interfaith marriage has been profiled in national media. He writes often for *America: The Jesuit Review* in the United States, and *The Tablet* in the United Kingdom. Sweeney is also the publisher at Paraclete Press in Massachusetts. He sits on the governing board of The Lux Center for Catholic–Jewish Studies at Sacred Heart Seminary and School of Theology (Hales Corners, Wisconsin), the only center of its kind housed at a U.S. Catholic seminary, to whom all the royalties for this book are being donated.